The E

Certainty

How To Thrive When Playing By The Rules Is A Losing Strategy

SIMON DUDLEY

THE END OF CERTAINTY

*How to Thrive When Playing
by the Rules Is a Losing Strategy*

ISBN 978-1-61961-343-0

LIONCREST
PUBLISHING

*To Mimi, who has always
had more faith in me than I
had in myself. Thank you for
helping me believe in myself.
You are my world.*

CONTENTS

Introduction

Re-Inventing the Wheel

In 1890, my great-grandparents owned a business in Islington, North London which built carts. Eighty percent of the cost of making these carts went towards the wooden wheels. If you didn't make a wooden wheel perfectly round, and if the axle wasn't set dead in the center, you'd never sell another one. Your customers would be wobbling down the road. It was hard to make perfectly round wheels back then, but my great-grandparents were masters of the craft.

For anyone who wanted an industrial-style cart, my family's workshop was the place to go. They would rent their carts—horse-drawn and hand-drawn models—to everyone from rag-and-bone men to milk delivery services. This market worked well, and my family became wealthy. At one point, they had over a million pounds (in modern money) that they kept in the house. At one particularly big wedding, there was a breadbasket literally stuffed full of "white fivers"—white five pound notes about the same size as standard letter-sized American paper.

Then, a historic event changed everything for my family: Henry Ford created the Model T.

Others soon followed suit, inventing their own automobiles. The people who had been buying and renting carts started buying trucks or small cars instead. Despite my family's expertise in their craft, nobody wanted a car with wooden wheels. Very quickly, within the space of 10 years, their business started to collapse. The number of people making wooden wheels stayed the same, but the number of people who needed them dropped dramatically. The price of wooden wheels plummeted.

By 1930, only 15 years after their heyday, the family business had collapsed to the point where they were living in abject poverty in King's Cross in London. They would have to sell a chair so that they could eat for another few days. Their circumstances were so grim that only the full employment of the Second World War rescued them from poverty.

The family workshop is a perfect example of a thriving business that, due to a revolutionary event, went from top of the market to bankruptcy in 15 years. *This happens all the time in business.* The funny thing is that if these business-killing revolutions don't affect us directly, we often barely notice they're happening. This is unfortunate because when we're aware of these massive changes, we can take steps to avoid them—and capitalize on them.

In my family's case, if they had seen the first car on the road and realized, "Oh my word, that's going to change everything," they could have taken the most obvious action: They would have sold the wooden wheel business to someone who hadn't seen the future coming.

My great-grandparents would have gotten top dollar for their business. Then they could have gone off and done whatever else they wanted with that money. To give you an idea: That family wedding where white five pound notes were overflowing from a breadbasket? The money that was casually left lying around the house that weekend could have bought 20 houses in Central London at that time, or been used as seed capital for their next venture.

* * *

My family's business collapsed because they failed to recognize a market-changing event—I call them *Excession Events*—that spelled their doom. An Excession Event occurs when what is considered to be "success" in a market changes. This inevitably creates scenarios where people think success in their market is defined by a certain set of criteria, but the market decides a completely new set of criteria is now what it wants. What success looks like can now be dramatically different.

Cell phones are another great example of how an Excession Event can change the criteria of success. Picture, if you will, the cell phone you had in the year 2000. You may have had a Motorola Razr flip phone, which was the most popular phone in the world that year. The market went crazy for these little flip phones. They defined what it meant to be a successful phone in 2000. Motorola sold over 450,000,000 of them.

Now imagine I climb into my time machine and visit you, back in 2000, with your little flip phone in hand. If I told you I was from the year 2015, and that I had the future's most advanced phone in my pocket, what would you think it looks like? You might guess that it would be smaller, because in 2000, phones had gotten smaller and smaller. The Motorola Razr was the ultimate incarnation of that. With that in mind, you might guess this phone from the future was the size of a credit card.

Next, you might think to yourself that battery life is getting longer and longer. Your Motorola Razr probably had a four or five day battery life. You might guess that by the year 2015, battery life would be a month.

Finally, you might think the phone of the future would be unbelievably tough. You might be able to throw them around, drop them, skip them across the parking lot, put them through a washing machine cycle or leave them on the roof of the car without a worry.

Of course, if in 2000 you visualized a phone from 2015 being small and indestructible with an amazing battery life, you would be completely wrong. The best-selling phone from the year 2015 is twice the size of the Motorola Razr, the battery barely lasts a day, and if you drop it, it's $300 to replace the screen.

Back in 2000 you might wonder how that's an improvement. The answer: The iPhone of today is a far better device than a Motorola Razr from 2000 because it has *redefined what success looks like*. We still call them mobile phones, but they're not really. They're now mini supercomputers. It just so happens that one of the apps on these mini-supercomputers is a phone.

What Apple achieved with the iPhone redefined an entire market, rendering flip phones obsolete. And they did it in about the same period of time that Henry Ford did it to the horse and cart industry.

✳︎　✳︎　✳︎

These Excession Events impact a lot more than just technology. They reshape society. When I started working back in 1986, I sold fax machines, dictation equipment, typewriters and word processors. I was just on that cusp of change, where many people bought typewriters which would cost significantly more than a good, decent laptop would in the modern era. In modern money, it could be $1,500 to $5,000 for a typewriter.

A word processor, at that time, was a little box that sat on the side of the typewriter with a nine-inch display and a five and a quarter inch floppy disk. It had a single 76K floppy disk. You would type onto the keyboard and it would come up on the seven-inch screen. There were no fonts, no bold, and no italics. It was all command code so you needed specialist typists. Once the letter was written and they were happy with it, they'd press the print key and then the letter would be printed at 12 characters a second on a daisy wheel printer. It was amazing and magical to the people who used to typewriters.

In today's money, these word processors would cost you $15,000 to $25,000. Relatively few organizations bought them, and they were typically operated by professional typists who could type between 70 to 95 words a minute flawlessly.

By modern standards, I've never met anyone in the last 10 years who could type that fast. The reason why? PCs started coming out, and they were getting cheaper and cheaper—somewhere between $5,000 and $7,000. Better still, starting in 1991, when Microsoft Office launched, PCs came packaged with the ultimate word processor: Word.

Word, as part of Microsoft Office, was much better than these dedicated word processors. It was cheaper and you could do other things on it, like spreadsheets. It ran in Windows and it was relatively intuitive, so you didn't need a training course to work out how to use it. You could move your mouse to the bold button and click "bold," and then it would type on the screen in bold. Not a big deal in the modern era, but at the time it was utterly revolutionary.

Microsoft Word was an Excession Event that redefined what

success looked like in a word processor. A word processor, suddenly, was not about high-quality typists typing faultless work at lightning speed. It was about everybody typing their own letters.

How did this shape society? Secretaries went away. And that was just the beginning.

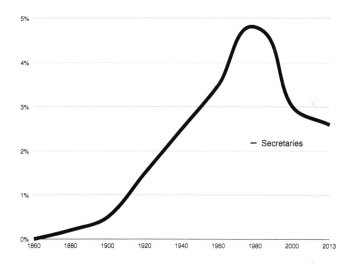

When I first started work in the late 1980s, I used to visit local insurance companies to sell them fax machines. There would be 200 women in the office typing pool, all in rows, all with their own desk, all facing the front where the matronly headmistress would be checking everybody's work. The typists would have two trays: the "in" tray and the "out" tray.

And all day, they would compulsively move work from one tray to the other.

By 1995, all of those people were gone. There were no typists. Instead, most people had PCs on their desks and everyone started typing at five words a minute. The number of mid-level executives who stabbed their keyboards with one finger for the next 10 years was shocking, and awful to watch.

Along with Word, Excel and PowerPoint caused their own business-killing Excession Events that rendered other positions practically obsolete. Harvard Graphics was a company that owned 86% of the presentation market during the DOS era. After Windows came out, they were crushed by PowerPoint in two short years. Suddenly you didn't need spreadsheet jockeys or graphics jockeys or entire bureaus to go and do that type of work for you. Everyone could just use the standard, off-the-shelf PowerPoint template, stick in their own data, and be done.

Because of these technologies, the number of "spreadsheet jockeys" went up, but the quality of each one went down. The number of "graphic designers" went up, because everyone became one, but the quality of each one went down. The quality of typing fell through the floor because everyone was now typing. All the past professional typists were now doing something else. Introduction of these software programs had transcended business, and had changed the very fabric of society. It also empowered a generation of women to be much more than typists. It changed society.

* * *

It's unlikely that I would be writing a book about these Excession Events, let alone any type of book. I have dyslexia, which made school a challenge. But ultimately, and perhaps counter-intuitively, my learning disability shaped me in a way that empowered me to recognize Excession Events ahead of time.

Before the age of five, every single photograph there is of me shows me squinting into the distance. I was horribly short sighted. As a result, I couldn't even see the blackboard at school. No teacher had noticed until then, which, in itself, is a little disturbing.

By the age of seven, I had glasses—but I still couldn't read, due to dyslexia. The school system where I lived in southern England didn't believe in dyslexia. They said it didn't exist; it's all in the mind. The bigger reason may have been that Britain, in the 1970s, was in a catastrophically horrible financial position. Britain had to be bailed out by the IMF in 1976, and certainly didn't have the resources to help a slow-learning kid with dyslexia. My public school wasn't going to help me. Instead, my parents found an independent organization to help me. By the age of eight, I could read thanks to some techniques they taught me.

At the age of 11 your academic future was set. Britain had grammar schools and trade schools. The top 20% of students went to the grammar school while the remainder went to trade school. Against all odds, I passed the grammar school entry exam, also known as the 11+ Exam, with flying colors.

But the school system rejected me. They said, "No, he's too young to go to the grammar school."

"Hang on. He's passed all the exams in spite of being too young, he's got an IQ that you've measured that's in the top 1%, and his math ability is that of a 15-year-old," my parents argued. "Why would you possibly reject him?" They had no good answer; just a dismissive reply that the school was full. They refused to change anything.

I remember sitting on the top of the stairs and seeing my mum in tears, shouting at someone from the education system who had just told her, "If you don't drop this, that you want your son in the grammar school, we will take him into care and we will mark you as unfit parents." And so it was decided: Despite acing the entry exams for grammar school, they were sending me to trade school. There was nothing we could do about it.

I've always had a problem with bullies. From the youngest age I remember, I got picked on. Very few kids wore glasses in my day, but I had glasses as thick as the bottom of jam jars. And from my earliest memory, the moment the big kid came along to try and bully me, I would smack him in the mouth as hard as I could.

When I saw this school bureaucrat bullying my mum, a new instinct kicked in. I said to myself, "I'm done. I want nothing to do with you people." I realized that if you played the game by other people's rules, then you're at their mercy. I also realized that your standard off-the-shelf education system can have some major downsides if you don't fit within a certain box. At that point, I made the decision to say "screw authority." I became a contrarian.

* * *

As distraught as my mum was over our treatment by the school, my father seemed less concerned. In his world, we were a family of "unqualified successes." He just didn't believe very much in the education system, even though he was a top scientist in what he did. I believe my contrarian nature may have come from him.

My father was born in 1935. In 1951, it was his time for National Service, which was conscription in Britain; this meant you had to serve in the Armed Forces. My father had no interest at all in becoming an infantryman, but he had done nothing useful at school. His father was a furrier and his mother ran the Women's Conservative Association for London during the war. They were business people, but not remotely technical or science-minded.

My father decided he wanted to be in radar, though he could never remember why. He certainly wanted to be in the Royal Air Force (RAF). He'd built and flown model aircrafts from the age of six or seven. He joined the RAF at the age of 18, committing to four years of service in order to be placed in radar.

He started learning how all the technology worked, and very quickly became "third line support," which is the highest level. In this third level, he would bring the technology or the product back, work out what was wrong with it, and fix fundamental problems. He did this for four years, and then left to work in Telecoms in Northwest Kent near London. From there he moved to Philips in the late '50s. At that point his career really took off. He was designing the early days of computer-based circuit simulation.

By the end of his career in the mid '80s, he had 50 engineers working for him. Every one of them had a first-class honors degree from one of the top universities in the country. He was doing work on the effects of nuclear weapons on electronics. He was involved in lots and lots of different, interesting projects involving lasers and atom smashers and all sorts of things that he wasn't allowed to talk about. But remarkably, my father had no "education" and no "qualifications" at all. He just wanted to do the work.

Perhaps that's why, when I passed my 11+ Exam and was inexplicably rejected by grammar school, my father became so angry. I remember after one Parents-Teachers night, my father came home furious. He said he hated schools and he hated teachers. He would actually turn to these teachers and say, "Those who can, do. Those can't, teach. Those who can't teach, teach gym." And most infuriating to him of all, when he would ask teachers about my performance, and they would complain and say, "He's not a good student. He asks too many questions."

I believe my father was proud that I was not the compliant, happy student who would blindly accept the teacher's word as an absolute authority. I never accepted *anyone's* authority. I refused to give respect just because of someone's title. I gave respect because of what someone had done lately. If they hadn't done anything useful lately, then my level of confidence in them—as well as my respect for them—fell away. In school, I wasn't being educated. My favorite classroom activity became watching the seagulls on the field patting the grass to get the worms to come up.

Meanwhile, my school placed great emphasis on pride, and before all else, compliance. This did not bode well for me, because of my contrarian attitude. I fell right through the bottom of the school. I dropped out of school at age 18 and never looked back. If my father could be an "unqualified success," then surely I could, too.

I am thankful for my school career, however unpleasant it may have been. After my experiences in education, I came to resent the idea of people telling me what the right answers were. I didn't have any faith in their system. And so I developed and sharpened a contrarianism that has allowed me to question the world, and therefore assess the world much more accurately. This has empowered me to see Excession Events and watch them unfold up close. By pure luck I have also witnessed a number of Excession Events in my own career.

* * *

To recognize Excession Events when we see them, it helps to have a grasp of how history works. People may try to deny Excession Events by saying, "Oh, no, no. Changes as dramatic as that couldn't possibly happen." I just look at them and say, "It has happened in the past." History shows that these events have happened quickly, too. People in the past lived through enormous changes and survived. There were big winners and big losers because of these inevitable changes.

Unfortunately, one of the first lessons of history is that people don't learn from history. People look at what has historically happened within a specific context in order to extrapolate what will happen next. This rarely works, because the future is not linear—and Excession Events, which have always been a part of history, can be extremely disruptive to our projections of the future.

A perfect example of this would be the horse-and-cart world versus the new world of self-driving cars. In 1894, there was a major crisis in London and New York because the horse manure problem was becoming so extreme that they didn't know what to do with it. New York had 100,000 horses and 1,250 tons of horse manure taken off the roads every day.

Dead horses were left at the side of the road to rot. If you left them to rot for a few weeks, they were easier to cut up and cart away. As a result, the air quality and the general sanitation of big cities like New York and London was awful, with the potential to get much worse. People of the time looked back at history and extrapolated that by the year 1940,

London streets would be in "deep shit," quite literally: Nine feet deep of it a day, to be exact.

Of course they weren't fools for thinking this way; they were working with the data that they had available at the time. They didn't understand that in 1894, Henry Ford was just thinking about how to automate car manufacturing. If you'd shown anyone in 1894 a car, like the Mercedes tricycle, and said, "Don't worry. In 20 years all your horses and carts will all be replaced by this sort of thing," they would have looked at you like you were mad. But sure enough, within 40 years of 1894, there were no horses on the road. If you'd said that to anyone in 1894 they would not possibly have believed you.

When cars first started appearing on the roads, people thought that they would use them in the same *historical* way they had used horses, just with a motor instead of a horse. But in reality, the car fundamentally changed everything about how a transport system works. As a major Excession Event, the advent of cars changed the criteria of success for transportation—a shift that expanded to trigger many significant societal changes that we now take for granted.

One example of a major change that people completely forget ever existed: What happened to all the blacksmiths? Think how many blacksmiths New York had in 1890; they numbered in the thousands. What happened to the livery boys, or the people producing all the hay that fed the horses? What happened to the horse manure shovelers? When all those jobs were decimated by cars, well, what happened to them all?

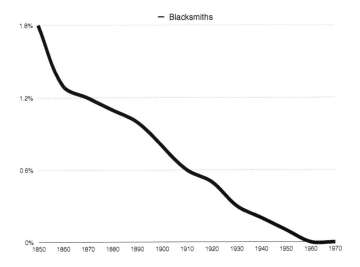

If any of these workers had tried extrapolating from history to determine their future, it would have looked bright indeed, with abundant horses to feed, horseshoes to smith, and manure to shovel. But when you look at meta-history, it becomes clear that this type of thinking doesn't work. We can't think about history as a linear timeline that we can extrapolate the future from. A big part of the reason why is because Excession Events—these powerful, unpredictable X factors—can change things in ways we never could have imagined.

❊ ❊ ❊

So what are the negatives of Excession Events if you don't handle them properly? As we've seen in the examples so far, your entire raison d'etre, your whole reason for having a job or a career or a business, can just simply cease to exist. You need to be in a position where everything that you think is reasonable may go away. The whole premise of your company or your individual career could just simply evaporate.

The good news: There are tremendous positive gains to be had when Excession Events occur, if you take the lessons in this book to heart. With the right awareness, you may "see the future" and make decisions ahead of the curve. You can capitalize on changes and push the world forward more than others who wait. You can invest in a way that means that you're more likely to benefit from other people coming up with good ideas that you saw early. You can also get out of the top of a market that's about to crash. You can have more time than anyone else to retrain for what the new world looks like. You can hedge both personally and professionally against potential threats from all angles.

My grandfather, my father's father, was a fur trader who exemplifies how to capitalize on an Excession Event. Fur was very popular until the '70s, at which point fur became, for whatever reason, murder. People didn't like the idea of wearing furs. There were many people who had paint thrown on them, particularly in London. In Europe it wasn't a problem; but in London especially, the backlash against fur became just ridiculous. All of the sudden, you mustn't be nasty to minks. Cows, pigs and chickens were fine to be appalling to, of course.

My grandfather, recognizing this Excession Event would

bring great changes to his fur-trading company, decided to shift gears. He began doing consulting work with a company that made "faux" fur fabric. He understood the faux fur fabric was going to replace real fur, and that manufacturers had a specific need to be filled: They didn't know how to make fake fur that looked like real fur. The early fur fabrics were horrible, nasty imitations. You could definitely tell it wasn't real. But today you can wear fur fabric that feels and looks just like real fur. Part of the reason for that is the work my grandfather did. Because he recognized a looming Excession Event and adapted his business accordingly, my grandfather continued to prosper while other furriers shut their doors forever. I should point out my grandfather was no chemist and knew nothing of the technology on which his work was based.

Another example is that some of today's car manufacturers actually started as bicycle manufacturers that saw the opportunity of moving into cars. Both Peugeot in France and Skoda in Czech Republic started as bicycle manufacturers in the 1880s. Peugeot still makes bicycles, but they realized the market opportunity of making cars was far greater. Both of those companies built cars for the people, not expensive cars. They weren't building Rolls Royce or Bentley equipment. They were building normal vehicles that your average man could afford to buy, and went on to take a large share of that market.

With the advent of the automobile, some other early coach building companies, like Cadillac and Lagonda, realized that they were actually in the luxury business. It was irrelevant whether their coach was being towed by a horse or driven by an internal combustion engine. They understood that their business was building comfortable, luxurious solutions for their clients. As a result, the automobile Excession Event that could have destroyed them instead launched them to incredible success.

*   *   *

There are countless examples of businesses that were decimated by Excession Events, and businesses that, by anticipating these events, thrived in their wake. This book is written to help you and your business succeed— by teaching you three important strategies in Excession Event management.

You will learn to understand that Excession Events may be unpredictable in their form, but utterly predictable in their inevitability. To understand that these events even exist, and that they occur all the time, is an important first step. But they cannot be extrapolated from where we are today. That's the first key to understanding Excession Events. You cannot steer by your wake.

Imagine Excession Events as tsunamis. If you didn't know tsunamis occurred, ever, what would you not do? You wouldn't put the alarms up. You wouldn't put any people on the beach on towers. You wouldn't put any flood defenses in. You would simply blindly carry on with your life right until the point where it suddenly went under 25 feet of water. In that respect, just knowing that Excession Events exist is a significant part of the battle.

Secondly, you will learn how to mitigate the risk of Excession Event changes. There are so many useful steps to take, for you personally and for your business, that can help reduce your risk. For example, working to understand what business you're truly in, diversifying your knowledge, and diversifying your business. These steps help as you try and do everything you can to hedge against a single Excession Event taking out your business completely.

Finally, we will discuss strategies on how to take advantage of Excession Events' unexpected upheavals, and potentially turn them into massive gains. If you can see far enough ahead, you can retrain or you can change your business faster than anyone else. You can take advantage of the new set of criteria for success, and you can win.

In truth, over history, the number of winners created by Excession Events has always been far greater than the number of losers, but only over a protracted period. I'm sure that wheelwrights in the 1920s had a terrible time of it, but the number of car mechanics that worked between 1940 and the year 2000 probably eclipsed them by a factor of 20. There's a tremendous advantage in understanding how a market can change and placing yourself in a position to surf that wave. This book will help you get there.

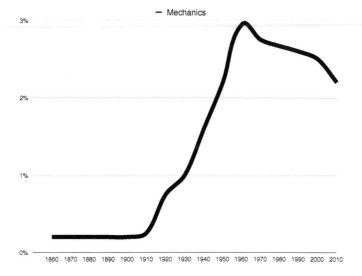

It is important to note that this book does not contain any oracle-like predictions or prescriptions to eliminate future risk. You can't turn to the back page of the book and say, "The answer is this." It isn't about that. Excession Events are more like exercise: Doing the right things on a consistent basis will help you survive and thrive. There's no magic bullet, no pill to take.

This book cannot tell you when the next rogue wave is coming, or from what direction. Instead I am suggesting you stick some klaxons up and a couple guys on the beach on a tower with binoculars. The book is about how to do that intellectually: It is a manual on how to deal with a world that is inherently full of risk. You don't have to be a genius to see these things coming. But if you follow the knowledge outlined in the pages that follow, you'll certainly seem like a genius when the next big Excession Event hits.

And the real beauty of the principles in this book is that they are timeless. Whether you are reading this book in 2015 or 2115, the principles are the same. This fact is important. Excession Events have always happened, but the speed at which they are happening is now increasing. They are increasing because the speed of innovation of our culture and our society is increasing. Instead of one big tsunami wave, these accelerating changes are creating lots of rogue waves. They're constantly coming, and unless you prepare now, the next one might sweep you and your business away.

PART ONE

The Emperor Has No Clothes

ONE

A Million Mouths

Although the human mind tends to work in a linear fashion, our growth is usually exponential. To give you a sense at the speed in which human society is growing, let's examine agriculture and sustenance as a useful analogy of human development. For humans, subsistence level—which is the minimum required to feed and sustain a person—is considered by the UN to be about $400 a year. It took humankind about one million years to get the point where we could feed a million mouths; where we could reach this subsistence level for that many people.

The next major Excession Event was farming, which manifested in multiple places around the world simultaneously. Around 5,000 BC, once farming was established as a concept, we increased the rate at which we could feed another million people at subsistence level to about 200 years. We went from a million years to 200 years in a less than a thousand years.

Fast forward to the post-Industrial Revolution era, in the world economy as it is today. We now feed another million mouths, in economic terms, every 90 minutes. In 7,000 years, we've gone from a million mouths every million years to a million mouths every 90 minutes. Today, we can feed another million mouths on the planet in actual food terms every 10 days. This rate of increase in the wealth of human society is just incredible, and it continues to increase.

If you were to grow the world economy at the same rate it has grown over the last 50 years on average, by the year 2050 the world will be 4.8 times richer than it is today. And by the year 2100 it will be 35 times richer than it is today, which is mind-boggling. Not every individual will be 35 times richer, of course. But certainly, the end of poverty in any meaningful sense, as we know it today, is absolutely going to happen. The scale of the society we would have built by that point is just inconceivable. But it's happening right now: The world will change more in your lifetime than in the last 2,000 years combined.

If you lived 500 years ago in an English village, you probably died in the house you were born in. You never went more than seven miles from your house. The only education you got was what the priests told you on a Sunday morning. You weren't plugged to any kind of world affairs. So even if you had an idea—and frankly the chances of you having one were pretty low because you weren't in a position to come up with one—who were you going to tell? Now, we're in a world where the most impoverished farmer is more connected than the President of the United States was in the Reagan era.

Statista, a consultancy, predicts cell phone penetration will rise from 4.4Bn users in 2013 to 5.47Bn by 2018.

Why are these exponential leaps happening? Consider that a thousand years ago, or even a hundred years ago, if you came up with a good idea on one part in the world, chances are it never got heard of anywhere else—either in your own village, or across the country, or across the world. Very few people in past times were in a position to have the opportunity to just *think*. Even if they did have the opportunity to think and be educated by all the giants that came before them, there was virtually no chance that their message would get out to the rest of the world.

What the Internet is doing, and what our society is developing now, is a fundamental change where if you have a good idea, it's probably going to get out there. It isn't true for everybody, but it is true for a lot more people than it used to be.

To be exceptional 500 years ago, you probably had to be the best out of 100 people in the village that you lived in. 100 years ago, you had to be the best in the city that you lived in, which might have 100,000 people. Today, the only way to be the best in the world is to be better than *everybody*. If you want to include those people who were actively on the Internet, today it is about two billion, and soon will be 5 billion. You've got to be a lot more than just pretty good. You've got to be the best.

As the scale of competition grows, however, so does the scale of collaboration—which takes us to Metcalf's Law. Dr. Metcalf was the man who invented Ethernet back in 1973. He started the company 3Com. He made a lot of money, and he's now a professor at the University of Texas. He stated that the utility of a network goes up at the square of the number of nodes in it. Now, what that means is this—the more people in a network, the more powerful it becomes at an exponential, or a square, rate.

So if there are two people in a phone network, the power of that network is four. If there are three phones, then it's three squared, so the power of the network is nine. As the phones increase in number from four to five to six, the power of that network become massive very quickly.

A perfect example of this would be Facebook. Facebook was really of very limited use when the early people on it were a few college students at Harvard and MIT. But the more people who joined it, the more people were attracted to it. At the time of writing (mid 2015) there are close to 1.5 billion Facebook users globally.

The thread that runs through all these ideas is that systems and societies are more powerful than individuals, and we've got bigger societies today than we've ever had. Not just in the sense of cities and more powerful countries, but ultimately as the most powerful global society: The World Wide Web. As technology enables our growing global population to connect, we multiply the very power of humankind exponentially.

This multiplying power directly affects Excession Events.

People are thinking of Excession ideas all the time. But throughout most of history, their ideas never went anywhere. Now, the power of our human network has been multiplied. And every piece of solid evidence suggests that, over time, the rate at which Excession Events will start occurring will increase, even more than it already has.

These Excession Events also typically come in waves, rather in a steady progress. Why does this happen? These waves of progress are often attributed to the power of converging technologies, which multiply their power to spark major fundamental changes.

Today, we may come up with a new idea and refine it until it gets better and better and better. We keep refining, right until the point when what success looks like is changed, typically by a series of ideas coming together. In the earlier cell phone example, cell phone advancements could only happen because numerous technologies came together. Interestingly, these technologies came together from many different people simultaneously. Everyone thought they had been copied by somebody else, which just isn't true. It is more accurate to say the opportunity for something to be invented that was brand new could only come to pass when other advancements had happened. When the pieces were in place and a series of new technologies had been invented, then it was inevitable that someone—and often multiple people—would package those ideas together.

Nothing is capable of stopping an idea whose time has come. Once the building blocks are there, it's just one more step to add the last piece that holds these ideas together into a functional form. This illustrates that although our thinking may be linear, when we combine it with additional external factors, including the ideas of other people, our thinking becomes a powerful multiplier.

❊ ❊ ❊

In 1964, Gordon Moore, one of the founders of Intel, stated that you would be able, for the same cost, to produce twice as much computing power every 18 months to two years. This assertion, which has come to be known as Moore's Law, has been true from 1964 until now. It appears that it's still going to be true, at least for the foreseeable future. This may seem obvious and inevitable, but it's neither. The guys at Intel don't just sit there and say, "We'll plant this chip in a pot of soil and let it grow into the next generation of processors." It doesn't work like that.

What happens is that they *believe* Moore's Law to be true. As a result, they build new technologies all of the time that happen to produce a result that seems to be Moore's Law at work. There is an argument that Moore's Law is actually holding them back. Because they believe in it so strongly, and adhere to it so closely, they're not making the 10× geometric growth opportunities that may be possible. Instead, they're thinking, "This machine needs to be twice as good as the last."

What's really happened is, to a large extent, "twice as good" has translated into processors simply getting smaller. They're not getting twice as fast every 18 months. The advancement of chip technology may look linear, but if you were to speak to an Intel engineer, he would laugh at you and say, "Well the effect is linear," but there are lots and lots of things that go into each one. Moore's Law may look like steady progress, but in truth it is a series of completely new technological advancements that continually reinvent how things are done.

Besides processors, most inventions are refinements of existing ones, and, therefore, they are additive. But occasionally, and with increasing frequency due to our internet-empowered age, you have ideas that have sex with other ideas and multiply. These ideas produce a much bigger difference, because, in the spirit of Metcalf's Law, they're multiplying two numbers together. These ideas are combining their DNA to produce something exponentially more powerful.

If we imagine technology as the ocean at the beach, we may see all of these new ideas coming in as a series of waves. But when you zoom out and look at what's happening from a macro level, these little waves add up to a sea of change: The tide comes in. Of course, not all of these idea-waves trigger global change. But every so often, conditions will be just right to produce an unusual outlier idea—a rogue wave—which then hurtles towards shore with the force of a tsunami.

Although these rogue Excession Event waves have always occurred, the rate at which they're happening is speeding up dramatically. Changes occur in waves that parallel with technology—and technology is advancing exponentially, producing staggering growth.

There are a finite number of ideas that folks will come up with in any period of time. But with more people who are more connected to a larger global network where they can bounce ideas off each other, and then the chances of a new idea coming to life increases all the time. As we've already seen from the growth of our society, the number of people in it and the number of ideas surrounding it is just going up and up. Therefore, the chances of two ideas randomly hitting each other and becoming an Excession Event by multiplying the two ideas together—or numerous ideas multiplying together—*has* to be increasing.

BLACK SWANS

When the English explorers first went to Australia, they discovered something that they couldn't possibly have conceived of: Black swans. Everyone *knew* that swans were white. The Englishmen who first saw those swans couldn't conceive that a swan could be black, and would have told you it was impossible until they saw it. This is an example of how people believe the universe works in a certain way until something comes along to prove to them wrong. After your worldview has been changed to a black swan, you see the world differently. Today, the probability of "black swans" is as low as ever, but we're rolling the dice far more often. Think of it as molecules bouncing around in a gas. What we've got now is much more gases in the same space, so the pressure increases. The ideas then bounce around more, and are much more likely to connect with another one. You could have a great idea in Boston, and I could have had a great idea in Texas. On the grounds that we had never met, those two ideas would never have sex and take off. But today, I could put something on the Internet, you could find it, and then we could be off to the races. Traditionally, Excession Events come from numerous ideas coming together. I suspect, in the future, they will become more sophisticated because they'll have more ideas that will come together at the same time. There are just simply more ideas out there.

The risk created by accelerated innovation is that people, and ultimately society, will simply fail to keep up. The rate of change will erode the foundations of society faster than it can absorb new ideas. This causes problems because our societal framework is designed to handle percolating new ideas at a relatively low rate. That's why societies—law, religion, social norms—work at a lower, slower rate than individuals within the society. If we get to a point when a society is changing at an enormous rate—i.e., large, successive Excession Events—then it stands to reason that society can get into enormous trouble. These tensions cause issues such as the culture wars so evident in the United States.

TWO

Blockbuster's Blunder

Companies and individuals who ignore Excession Events—and the changes they bring—risk massive failure. In a world of slow evolution, sticking with the status quo is often a "safe" decision, but in a world of Excession Events (especially when more and more of them are happening with greater and greater frequency), sticking with the status quo is the most dangerous thing you can possibly do. The world is changing rapidly, and it's crucial to keep up.

One of the best examples of a company that *didn't* keep up is Blockbuster Video. Let me state right off the bat that this chapter is not intended to portray Blockbuster as fools. Oftentimes, *after* the Excession Event, people will second guess those people who didn't see the tsunami coming. They turn around with crystal-clear hindsight and say, "Those guys at Blockbuster were idiots." They weren't idiots. They were completely reasonable, legitimate business people whose business model became obsolete. Success in their market underwent a sudden and radical change and they failed to take advantage of it.

Blockbuster did not acknowledge the possibility that something else could come along and replace their business. Further, they didn't really understand what business they were in. So let's examine what could Blockbuster have done differently.

Blockbuster started out in the world of small fragmented video stores that sold or rented you videos. This was during the time of the Betamax/VHS war, when these formats were fighting for victory. When one format emerged as a consistent, single winner, *somebody* was going to be in a position to grow that market extremely quickly.

In the early days of video cassette rental, there were stores that did Beta and there were stores that did VHS. When the dust settled and only VHS remained standing, Blockbuster helped consolidate the market by buying up, overtaking and replacing all the small Mom and Pop video stores. Their advantage was that they were big and they could buy cheaper off the studios than the small Mom and Pop stores could.

Blockbuster built a strong brand, and they dominated the market as a result. They actually ran a very efficient business: They were a $5 billion business in 2002, while 10 years earlier, they didn't even exist. That's an impressive piece of rapid growth.

Blockbuster's model was so successful, that they set their

strategy in stone. "Our business is renting people cassettes," they said. "We will now extrapolate our business out to infinity." As a result, what they *didn't* do was to try and consider or understand what their true business was. They believed that they could steer their business by its wake, which we've established simply doesn't work when the criteria of success changes. Blockbuster was extrapolating a prosperous future from their prosperous past, and it severely limited their vision.

Blockbuster's first major blunder was they saw themselves as being in the "VHS cassette" business. They didn't understand that the VHS cassette was simply a delivery mechanism for something else. People didn't rent "cassettes." They rented movies! Therefore, Blockbuster was really in the business of delivering movies; VHS cassettes were simply the medium. Because Blockbuster missed this distinction, they failed to see that there was a whole new way of delivering movies on the horizon.

This fundamental change that Blockbuster missed actually went far beyond movies. In the 1990s, people first started downloading games over the internet, and then, music. Remember Napster? What Napster did with music was prove that you could take a digital song, stick it into a server or multiple servers using a bit torrent client, and distribute it widely.

Until about 2000, movies weren't even distributed in a digital format. No one could have done it before then. What Napster did—and then Skype, The Pirate Bay and Netflix—was take advantage of a series of technological changes that, until that point, had not existed. These included high-quality Internet connectivity; sufficient processing power for compression and decompression; digital formats; and sufficient storage capacity. If any one of these technological advancements were missing, the model would fail.

Blockbuster failed to see this set of parallel developing technologies, and therefore they failed to see what the effect of those could be. Napster, on the other hand, recognized the power of these parallel technologies, leveraged them, and ruined the music industry as a result. If Blockbuster had been more technically advanced and hadn't been just extrapolating out to infinity its existing business model, then they might have realized, "Hang on. If you can digitize and distribute music easily, why couldn't you do this with films?"

* * *

Blockbuster failed to recognize the business they were actually in: Giving people access to entertainment in the most convenient and efficient way possible. And even as they lost ground to Netflix, they didn't try to catch up.

If I'd been Blockbuster—and again, it's very easy to do this with hindsight—I'd have seen the Excession Event of digital delivery coming, and I would have sold the business. An entirely legitimate response to an Excession Event is to admit you can't compete and sell the business to someone who either thinks they can still compete, or who hasn't seen the

change coming. If you can recognize the Excession Event before they can, by even a few weeks, it makes a big difference

Another response to the Excession Event might have been for Blockbuster to set up a Netflix-like competitor. Netflix, of course, had two models: They had the DVD-over-the-mail model, which bizarrely only really became useful after the Internet got going; and they had the digital delivery model. Neither of these models were extraordinary or proprietary.

There's no reason to imagine that Blockbuster couldn't

have done the same thing. Blockbuster would have had a significant advantage. They already owned the brand for the industry. Everyone knew who Blockbuster was in 2002. But instead of innovating and capitalizing on their brand, Blockbuster played it safe: They just wanted people to go to their stores. Blockbuster was not a technology company; they did not see that their salvation could come from technology.

We all remember the drill: You used to go Blockbuster on a Saturday afternoon, and you'd say, "Right, what movie should we get?" You'd wander through the aisles. You'd pick a couple of movies and your partner picked a couple of movies. Then you'd have an argument, and you'd end up watching the movies your girlfriend wanted to watch. Blockbuster correctly believed your chances of renting numerous movies were higher if they already had you in the store. Plus, you'd be more likely to buy popcorn and ice lollies and all the other guff that goes with watching a film at home.

In the end, by playing it safe and focusing on dollars for ice lollies and one or two additional movie rentals, Blockbuster failed to capitalize on a massive fortune, there for the taking, by simply giving their customers what they truly wanted: Easy, convenient and efficient access to entertainment. In a world of slow evolution, Blockbuster's status quo approach would have been prudent. But in our world of Excession Events, status quo is the most dangerous thing you can possibly do.

Status quo is "safe" for these companies because every business has investors and stockholders and analysts and a whole litany of other people who want to know what next week, next month, and next year will look like. If you don't have a plan that tells your investors and your creditors and the world what your plan is, then they're not going to invest in you. No CEO can field these questions and say, "I don't know. We're in a position where anything can happen over the next two years." He wouldn't last until the end of the press conference if he said that.

As a result, we live in a world where people spend their lives expecting it to be linear. What else can they do? Companies have to have an "up and to the right" spreadsheet and graph of revenues, numbers of customers, and all the other good things that happen in business. Because not to do so would mean that you're not fit to be a CEO.

The trouble with that thinking is that people get blinded by it. Even though they know it's mad; even though we all know it's a facade and that it's not real. But because the market believes it, then the CEOs and the senior management of organizations get wedded to it. Therefore, everyone just builds a business model that's focused on merely being better than what we already are. This is the difference between a 10% change and a 10x change.

If challenged to be 10% better, any business can say, "I can probably squeeze 10% more out of my business by simply driving it a little harder. I'll make it slightly more efficient. I'll make my sales people work slightly harder. I'll make my marketing budget go a little further. I'll push on my advertising agencies." Most businesses are in a position where, by making these incremental changes, they can get a 10% better, more efficient business on an annual basis.

To put it another way, if I said to you, "Here's a 100-pound barbell. Can you lift that above your head?" You probably could. If I put 10 pounds more on it; you most likely could still lift it. Or at least you'd try. If I said, however, "The barbell is now 1,000 pounds," what are you going to do? You're not even going to bother trying. You're going to go and do something else. You're going to go and hire a forklift truck and use that to lift the barbell over your head. In other words, what you're going to do is *change the way that you think about the problem*.

The real issue with the linear business is that we slowly eke out a slightly better experience all of the time. Many of us feel we have to work this way due to stock markets and shareholders, investors, creditors and all those things. Instead, looking for 10× better results can produce much better results within organizations because you actually have to think differently rather than become a slightly more efficient version of what you do today. That's not what Blockbuster did. Blockbuster looked for 10% gains in extra video rentals and popcorn sales, instead of looking for 10× gains by adopting a digital delivery model.

In today's world, where the rate of change is increasing at an exponential rate, the whole idea of keeping up by simply sweating the business for another 10% has become a losing strategy. If you're not looking for dramatically different ways of doing your business, then you're probably in a position where somebody else will replace you. And really, that's a good thing for society.

Our society is based on the concept of constructive destruction. For new businesses to come into play, with new ways of thinking and more wealth to be created, we can't just continually sweat another 10% out of the business. These new businesses are actually doing society a favor by sweeping the old ones away. The resources being spent on a business model that was failing can then be redeployed to go into something more useful.

Blockbuster exemplifies this as well. There wasn't a cull of the staff at Blockbuster immediately after the company went bust. All those people went off to a dozen or a hundred other companies, hopefully, all of which have higher growth rate than Blockbuster did. Excession Events may be disruptive, wreaking havoc with individuals and society at large. But at a macro level, these fundamental changes are the only way we can move forward.

And so, eight years after its peak market cap of $5 billion in 2002, Blockbuster declared bankruptcy. They went the way of the dinosaurs, leaving fossils of VHS tapes in brightly branded blue-and-yellow plastic cases. Netflix is the Excession Event that killed Blockbuster, but that does not mean that Netflix has won. The market is still changing dramatically.

The number of companies who now compete with Netflix grows on a daily basis: Hulu, Apple Movies, Amazon and more. Big players want a piece of that market, and it's beginning to split into a number of channels. I don't know what the next Excession Event for movies will be, but make no mistake: There *will* be another change. Somebody else will come along and have their day in the limelight. Then eventually *their* idea will get replaced. It's continual. Every win is only temporary—we must always keep up, or be forever left behind.

THREE

The Tyranny of the MBA

Do you have an MBA? If you do, you're not going to like this chapter very much, because I contend they're simply not worth the paper they're written on anymore. I would go so far as to say that the MBA is a distinct disadvantage. I don't just mean to your student loan debt, I mean to society as well. By instilling so-called "knowledge," suppressing questions, encouraging groupthink, and teaching from stale data, the MBA culture leaves people incapable of managing change.

There is one common thread that ties together all people and companies who handle Excession Events badly, it is this know-it-all mindset programmed by the MBA machine. "Knowing" is dangerous because it defines what you can see and makes it hard to look at things differently—which is quite the opposite of the agile mindset that is needed excel during Excession Events.

The Hawaiian King is a man who runs his own world. He doesn't know of any other world besides the island he lives on and the ones near him. He's the king of all these islands now. He had a few other tribes that he had to subdue, but now they're all either dead or enslaved. His people are now digging out the latest terror weapons of their era: Wooden canoes. And they're busy building pyramids to the gods that they've decided to pray to; gods that are becoming more sophisticated as their society grows.

The Hawaiian King is on top of the world and everything is going his way. Suddenly, one day he looks outside into the bay, and there's a ship. But it's a strange-looking ship he's never seen before. It's made of some sort of metal. It doesn't have any sails, and steam is coming out on the top of it. These unusual-looking individuals step out of this ship and start telling him that his islands now belong to some far-off king that he's never heard of before. There is this piece of cloth they're sticking up on a stick, which is the new king's standard.

They've got these bright-eyed young men who are there to tell him about a new god that he's got to pray to. Oh and, by the way, this new king that he never knew existed an hour ago also demands tribute in the form of taxes on a regular basis. The Hawaiian King's reign has come to a full stop. Society as his people know it simply ends.

Of course, this Excession Event was entirely unimaginable

for the Hawaiian King. Before that iron boat arrived, he could not have even conceived of a scenario that could usurp his power so absolutely. The Hawaiian King knew everything... or so he thought.

This philosophy is a common thread between all the people and companies who do a bad job of handling Excession Events. They think they have all the answers, and focus on the status quo rather than asking valuable questions. I would argue that Excession Events prove time and time again that supporting the status quo is a losing strategy. Don't do that. Don't defend the position. Look to rip it down. Then if you can't, well, maybe the position is correct. But don't spend your life defending it.

Unfortunately, instead of teaching students *how* to think, the MBA culture teaches students *what* to think. This practice may doom them to failure.

We've gotten to the point where MBAs are a symptom of a culture that is obsessed with education and "knowing things." But in truth, knowing the answers isn't what matters. In the modern knowledge economy, knowing which questions to ask is what really matters. MBAs, by their very nature, are poor at this. At its worst, the MBA culture completely suppresses the value of asking questions. Whether you spent tens of thousands or hundreds of thousands of dollars, depending on if you went to Phoenix or Wharton, you'll have a false sense of knowledge with your MBA.

"I spent all this money on this piece of paper," you may say.

"I had all these people tell me that I was God's gift; that after I received my MBA, people would be beating a path to my door. They told me that they would give me all the answers that I would ever need to solve all of my business problems. Therefore, I know all the answers."

Of course you do. After all, you paid a large sum of money for someone to give you an MBA certificate that says, "Aren't you a clever boy?"

When you have this mindset where you think you know it all, you're then unlikely to say, "Everything I have done until this point is wrong, and I'm going to start again." Because effectively, you're then saying, "The work that I've done until now was a waste of money and time." Emotionally, most people are incapable of coping with that. They would rather support the status quo, even if in their heart of hearts they knew it was wrong. It is easier. As a result, the MBA breeds stewards of the status quo, rather than visionary rebels who are out to change the world for the better.

* * *

Even the knowledge that MBAs hold so dear may not be as strong as advertised.

MBAs are a little like Generals: They are really good at fighting the last war. The MBA course is written and then it's taught. But it's not taught the same day it's written, as soon as it's written, it's out of date. In most business courses, and

MBAs are an extreme example of this, you end up with data that's well proven by long association with professors who looked at the data long ago. The MBA does not change dramatically on a weekly basis, *but the world does.*

Because MBA students are learning the last war's lessons, they often come to the wrong conclusions for the present day. As ill-equipped as this knowledge may be for the present, it's even less useful for the future: The next war simply isn't going to look like last one.

A perfect historical example of this is the French, who, after the First World War, understood that Germany remained a threat. To neutralize this threat, the French built the ultimate set of trenches all along where the Germans had come in during the First World War. At the time, this seemed like a brilliant move: They poured concrete and installed enormous Navy guns, creating what they thought to be the perfect defense.

The problem was, the Germans had come up with new ideas, mobile mechanized cavalry and Blitzkrieg (lightning war), which completely overwhelmed the French defenses in 10 days. The Germans had learned the lessons of the future, while the French acted on the old lessons of the past. MBAs are exactly the same: They learn from old results that leave them ill-equipped to manage future unknown challenges.

* * *

To prepare for Excession Events, we must always remember that answers have a half-life. What is true now won't be true in 40 years, even for the same question. Regardless, people get wedded to a question and answer combination that doesn't change.

Fifty years ago, if you'd asked how animals in different continents could look so similar but be thousands of miles apart, people would tell you about land bridges, where at some point in the distant past those creatures crossed. It was knowledge back then. *Now* we all know it was because of plate tectonics. But 30 years from now, are we certain the answer's *still* going to be plate tectonics? I don't know.

One of the problems with the education system is it sets in your mind the answer to a question even though the answer could change. This happens all the time.

A perfect example, and try to answer quickly: How many planets are in our solar system?

If you answered nine, it's because that's what you were taught. But you'd be wrong. There are eight planets in our solar system, and it's been that way since 2006. So even what we *know* isn't always true.

One of the fundamental problems with the education system as we have it today is that people have this concept that when they're young, they learn. And when they're older, they don't. That is wrongheaded for several reasons. One, because when you're young, you only learn the answers, not the questions.

Two, because the longer ago school was for you, the more likely it is those answers are wrong, because facts change over time. Three, because if you believe that when you went to school, you learned, and when you went to work, you didn't learn, then you end with a situation where you've decided you don't want to learn anymore.

I used to work with a woman who was an MIT graduate who once asked me about PowerPoint. I don't use PowerPoint, I use KeyNote. She looked at me and said, "I don't know how to use Keynote, so I have to use PowerPoint." I looked at her and said, "Did you come out of the egg knowing how to use PowerPoint?" Her response was fascinating. She looked at me and said, "Well, no. But I learned how to use PowerPoint ages ago. I *do things* now; I don't *learn* things." Shockingly, this was a mind that had received an MBA from MIT.

* * *

Finally, in addition to instilling a false sense of knowledge—and questionably outdated knowledge at that—the MBA often teaches "groupthink."

Groupthink teaches MBA students to not be contrarians, because contrarians are lonely outsiders. They teach that it's much better to be in with the in-crowd who come up with an idea for an organization. It doesn't matter that their idea is out-of-date or trite; it will still color everyone's opinion because of groupthink.

Here's how groupthink works. Organizations hire people who look like themselves. They bring in people with the same background, same education and same prejudices. If everyone is the same, you end up with a pecking order within the organization that's far too based on compliance to the existing status quo. The system will reward those who do the linear things that got the business to where it is today. It will promote the people who have linear thinking and exclude those who don't. The organization becomes homogeneous, and may even weed out all the contrarians who don't think like the group does.

This approach creates a shallow "gene pool" for the company, which just gets worse over time as the same people rehash the same ideas.

Most of American business culture today is infested with this MBA groupthink mindset. That's why so many companies are very good at pulling out another 10% out of an existing business model. But what MBA culture is *not* very good at is understanding that sometimes you need to do a 10× model change. This must be corrected in order for companies to survive their next Excession Event.

Thomas Jefferson said, "A man who knows nothing is closer to the truth than a man whose mind is full of half-truths and lies." And I think that sums up the sense of what an MBA degree, and its subsequent MBA company culture, can give us.

* * *

The groupthink problem is not limited to MBA. The whole education system is designed around a processor feeding you with facts and helping you understand how those facts fit together. What it doesn't help you understand is the significance of those facts.

We now live in a world where figuring out the right questions to ask is far more important than knowing what the right answers are. The Internet already has all the right answers. The trick is being good at working out which questions will uncover the best answers. Despite this, instead of teaching students how to ask questions, our education system loads them up with knowledge and all the danger it brings.

Institutions like the education system are created to change slowly and to hold back societal change in order to maintain consistency. Religious organizations exemplify this as well; they reward compliance to the existing order above all else. That's why they are so slow to change. In the meantime, everything else around us is speeding up. If you want to survive you've got to change faster. Those who are slow to change are much more vulnerable to Excession Events.

✻ ✻ ✻

In *War and Peace*, Tolstoy said, "We can know only that we know nothing. And that is the highest degree of human wisdom." With this simple statement, Tolstoy demonstrates a much better grasp of the reality of business, and life, than what you learn in getting your MBA.

Consider: How many of today's visionary business leaders are MBAs? Is Warren Buffet an MBA? No. Did Steve Jobs have an MBA? He didn't even have a degree. Did Bill Gates have an MBA? No degree. Does Sir Richard Branson have a degree? No. These visionaries never got caught up in a way of thinking. Like Tolstoy's observation, these greats are effectively "the simplest of men." Wherever the data took them, they went.

Meanwhile, the "well-learned" men already know the answers. If the data goes somewhere that disproves their answers, they are happier to give up the data than they are to give up their position.

In today's world, knowing the right answers is not a valuable skill. Any question I ask, I can simply perform a Google search on, and it will probably give me a fairly good answer, or it will certainly point me in the right direction. The advantage that Google will always have over you and me is that when you type into Google, "How many planets are in the Solar System?" It would have said, "Eight."

Now the number of facts in the world today is so extraordinary that you couldn't possibly learn any reasonable percentage of them. What you do learn is retained over a 10, 15, 20, 25, and 30-year period—but you don't update your information on an ongoing basis. Google does. Google updates its information a thousand times a second. Google is much more reliable than you are because with the data you've got, at best you are probably lucky if that data is right. And at worst, that data will send you off in completely the wrong direction.

You're never going to be better than Google, so why try? Instead, we should be focusing on what we can do that Google *can't* do—working out which questions to ask. I wonder if the right thing to do with the school system today would be, "Please write down 10 interesting questions." Not, "Here are 10 questions. Answer them."

Unfortunately, the education system is structured in a way that puts our young people through school, to a definitive end. School finishes; students, therefore, think that learning finishes. Students then graduate having absorbed lots of useless knowledge, but without having been taught the critical and valuable skill of *thinking*. And that is the worst possible scenario for our future.

THE SCOURGE OF THE CONSULTANT

Flaws in education and MBA studies often manifest in your garden-variety consultant. A consultant is a man who tells you the time with your own watch and then takes the watch in payment. They're the ultimate group-thinkers because they're always wedded to the status quo.

Consultants and analysts generally have a number of traits that are diametrically opposite to what a useful consultant would actually have. Very few of them are prepared to make a bold statement that would upset their client. Consultants are not, by their nature, wanting to be contrarian. Even though an outside, contrary viewpoint may be most valuable, and ultimately what the client really needs.

Instead, almost always, they will turn around to their clients and say, "I will tell you back what you want to hear. Because if I don't, you'll fire me and find another one." They want you to pay them more hours, more days for them to come around and say, "You should tweak this." They will often damn you with faint praise, which is just the worst. "You're all doing great. It's marvelous." They're cowardly, and they will never stand up to you—even if standing up to you will make the organization better.

The other thing I find with these folks is there's no common term of reference. They haven't lived in the organization or the individual's world before. So the only common term of reference is somebody else's previous world. And the problem with previous worlds is that that wasn't something that survived another Excession Event. So a little bit like the MBAs. They're fighting the last general's battle.

Worst of all, for outside consultants or analysts, there are no consequences for being wrong. That's why a great spot-test for a consultant or an analyst is to tell them you want them to invest. If they believe with absolute certainty that X is happening, have them put their money where their mouth is. Of course, they never will.

Consultants and analysts *do* have an ability to help organizations wring out better productivity; they can do the 10% improvement from time to time. But they're useless at the 10×.

If you are trying to prepare your business for Excession Events, you would be well advised to avoid consultants and analysts. They're great at breaking down the status quo, but they are incapable of seeing the world a different way because they're so wedded to the existing form that the market takes. They know more and more about less and less until they know everything about nothing.

On an ongoing basis, it's much better to know less and less about more and more so you could stand back and you could see how lots of things connect together and then that allows you to know nothing but about everything. To have the vision to affect 10× change is far more useful in today's world.

PART TWO

If You Do the Same Thing
You've Always Done

FOUR

The Aristotle Example

In the movie *Planet of the Apes*, Charlton Heston is talking to Dr. Zaius, who's the top guy for the apes, and he says, "This world is topsy-turvy." Dr. Zaius looks at him and says, "It's only topsy-turvy because you presently inhabit its lowest rung." Charlton Heston's character hated this because the status quo now meant he was at the bottom of society.

Most societies are built by the people who are at the top of it. Societies, therefore, generally become self-serving towards the people at the top. It's that institutionalization concept; the idea that, "I don't want to rock the boat because I'm doing all right on it." Most people are relatively happy with their position in life. That's why it's a basic fact that people do not like change! When things have changed historically, it hasn't turned out well for the common man. Change typically means chaos or even death. This is especially true of Excession Event-grade changes.

The Luddites are a perfect example of chaotic change. At the beginning of the Industrial Revolution, which started in Britain in the late 1700s, power looms started being put into these newfangled things called factories. This was an Excession Event triggered by James Watt's steam engine, which enabled faster processing of textiles. Next came new Arabian looms that were controlled with the feet. These factors massively accelerated textile production.

Before all this, it was a cottage industry. People worked from home, making individual sets of clothing. Making cloth was extremely laborious, but it paid well. People could live in these little cottages and be their own bosses. Every couple of weeks or every few months, someone would come along and pay them for their cloth.

When the new factory looms came out, they were anywhere between 20× and 50× faster. This triggered new events. Firstly, the price of cloth plummeted so that none of these people could afford to live in their little homes anymore. They couldn't afford to make cloth. Secondly, the only jobs available to them involved going to work for somebody else in a factory and being paid a pittance. A lot of people took offense to this and decided to smash the machines. This was called the Luddite Rebellion because of Mr. Luddite, one of the ring leaders.

The consequences for these Luddites were serious. A number of them were hanged and many deported. They lost the rebellion and the Industrial Revolution gained steam. For the Luddites, change was disastrous. As has been demonstrated time and again, society benefits but individuals are often crushed by dramatic change.

Another chaotic change example involves professional musicians in the 1930s, who got very upset when talking movies came out. Prior to that, there would always be orchestras of varying sizes in theaters that would play music along with the film. As soon as talking movies came out, the cinema started getting rid of the orchestras. There were many protests over this. Including this lovely poster:

AN ADVERTISING CAMPAIGN FROM THE AMERICAN FEDERATION OF MUSICIANS (SEPTEMBER 2, 1930 SYRACUSE HERALD)

The advent of talking movies was a disastrous change for professional musicians—a group who had less than a generation previously benefitted greatly from the advent of silent movies.

One last recent example of chaotic change was the uproar among taxi drivers in London, Berlin and many other cities. Uber was coming to these cities and the cab drivers were up in arms that their protected industry was going to be disrupted by newcomers. They think change is bad now? Wait until self-driving cars arrive. (We'll cover much more about this technological disruption later in the book.)

Change happens. Sometimes changes make big noises. And every time these changes happen, they create new chaotic changes, and opportunities.

Remember that Arabian loom? It triggered the next change: Cloth makers started running out of wool and cotton because they didn't have spinning wheels. And then, the spinning wheel arrived from China. Suddenly there was an awful lot more wool and material that you could then make cloth out of. Technological change came in stages. It wasn't luck that the spinning wheel arrived from China. Previously, the spinning wheel would have been a solution no one needed. It was only the introduction of the looms that instigated the search for a solution to another part of the supply chain.

Once you have looms from Arabia and the spinning wheel from China, the cost of cloth plummets by a factor of at least 50. As a consequence, there are a lot more linen rags available, as people don't hold onto their old clothes anymore. They instead start having multiple sets of clothing, rather than just one.

The consequence of cheaper linen rags is that paper becomes much, *much* cheaper. Johannes Gutenberg comes out with the printing press to take advantage of all this cheap paper. This made the cost of any printed material drop through the floor. Cheap printing without cheap paper would have been of very limited value. But once cheap paper and cheap printing were available everything changed.

The arrival of cheap printed matter next affected the Catholic Church. At the time, they were selling indulgences, which are effectively a theological IOU on sinning. If you paid the Church enough, they would give you a "theological get out of jail free" card for any sins that you may commit in the future. Indulgences enabled the rich to repent in advance, saving them time in purgatory after death. The bigger the sin you wanted to commit, the higher the cost. These indulgences were enormously profitable for the church, and one of the primary reasons there are so many fabulous churches across Europe dating from the 15th century.

With the arrival of cheap print, the Catholic Church quickly realized that they could start using this new wonder machine—the printing press—to print indulgences. This meant that the cost for the Catholic Church to produce indulgences dropped through the floor.

Everything was going swimmingly for the Church until it

upset a radical preacher in Germany, Martin Luther, who then stated that the Catholic Church was simply making money off people by absolving them of sin. This would have been a small theological debate in a rural corner of Germany, except that Martin Luther had access to a printing press, too. As a result, his message went "viral" across Europe. Within a month the story was all across Europe. Both Luther and the Church employed the printing press very effectively in this propaganda war. Very quickly, he became the world's first celebrity. Luther's agitation was the direct cause of the Reformation, a seismic split in European and world history.

This is a perfect example of a series of small technological changes and social changes that end up with something as enormous as the Reformation, which then kicked off the whole European Enlightenment, and the modern world.

✳   ✳   ✳

Changes can build and build, gaining momentum until they wipe out entire belief systems. Strangely, our response isn't to be sad or worried when change happens. More often, we pretend the change isn't even happening. We become paralyzed by dogma.

Aristotle once noted that people keep doing things long after the usefulness of those things has expired; long after the old model has been proven false. It is our nature to be this way. It seems to be in our DNA as the animals that we are.

My dogs will beg at the table because, at some point in the past, one of my kids gave them some food. They now associate begging at the table with getting some food. So they'll always beg, whether they get any food or not, because there is that *chance* it will happen. They believe that if they don't beg, they'll never get any food. So, they put a correlation between those two things together.

My favorite story of this concept is where, one Thanksgiving, a little girl is helping her mother in the kitchen. "Mom, I see you cut the ham in half. Why did you do that?" she asks her mother. "Oh, it's a family tradition. We cut the ham in half and we put one half in each oven," the mother replies. "We bought this house specifically because it had a double oven and it took us months longer than we thought it would to find a house that had a double oven." "But *why* do you cut the ham in half?" the daughter asks again. "Well, it's family tradition and we've always done that. I think it makes the food better or something, I don't really know the answer. Why don't you ask Grandma?"

The little girl goes and asks Grandma and says, "Grandma, why do you cut the ham in half?" "Well, that's a good question, dear," Grandma replied. "When your grandfather and I bought our house, we had to spend thousands of dollars extra changing the kitchen around to buy a double oven, because, after all, simply nobody had double ovens in those days. It was really painful, I remember, but it's a family tradition and we knew it mattered." The daughter asks again, "Well, *why* do you do it?" "Well, I don't really know," Grandma says. "I don't know, maybe it's something to do with the food being better or something. Why don't you ask your great-grandma?"

Great-Grandma is sitting in the living room and she's old and frail. The little girl goes up to her and says, "Great-Grandma, why does this family always cut the ham in half and cook it in two ovens?" She goes, "Well, I have no idea why my daughter and granddaughter do it, but I did it simply because the oven wasn't big enough."

This is a classic story of something being done long past the time of its usefulness. People do these things all the time, simply because they become dogmatic. The useless activity becomes something unconsidered. A dogmatic position is an unconsidered one. Our lives are full of these legacy cultural tails, and they are the societal equivalent of the appendix.

In business, and individually, we repeat the same actions and expect the same results, which is not unreasonable. What we *don't* look at is what the reasoning was in the first place. So we start making assumptions that we've done something in a certain way because it will produce a certain result, even if it's not actually connected. Correlation is not causation.

The correlation of cutting the ham in half has nothing to do with making the food better; it's to do with the fact that Great-Grandma didn't have an oven big enough.

There are lots of these examples. It's just how the world works. People hang on to a position without actually ever questioning it. So, they sit there and make the assumption that because we've done it this way, we'll always do it this way.

Certain South American tribes probably did human sacrifices because they killed someone in battle and suddenly the harvest was great the next year. Then, they killed a few more people and the harvest got better the next year. Then they thought, "Well, correlation is causation. So, the more people we kill, the better the harvest will be." After a while, they forget why they were doing it, but continued to do it anyway—because it would upset the gods if they didn't do it.

This way of thinking is fine—minus the human sacrifice part, of course—until your beliefs start informing incorrect decisions because you are stuck in old ways of thinking.

✻ ✻ ✻

In the business world, the old way of thinking is linear thinking: Companies will continue to do the same thing because they assume that doing the same thing slightly better will create a slight increase in the business they're already doing.

But actually, it's quite possible that there is no correlation between what they're doing and where their business is. They get themselves tied up in a situation where they don't know if it is or not. Many won't take the risk to find out. They never go back and ask the original question as to, "*Why* are we doing this?" They just do it out of habit.

Imagine you are a sales organization and you have a salesperson who produces $10,000,000 worth of business a quarter for you. Are you going to pay him $100,000 a quarter to do that business for you? The chances are yes, you are. However, there is absolutely no evidence to suggest this salesperson influences your business one way or the other. So, you pay him and the money comes in. But if you stop paying him, would the money come in anyway?

Businesses will avoid looking into this because if it's only $100,000 they pay to get $10,000,000, it's simply not worth upsetting the process. After all, it's only a 1% change. What if he did make a big difference to that end number? If you got rid of that salesperson, suddenly your revenue may drop by 10%. On the surface, you'd be $900,000 in the hole, and that would look like a very bad decision!

In reality, however, the cost of that sale typically goes up and up and up until it becomes close to the break-even point. But, because you've always done things in a certain way, you're not prepared to change anything because it's risky.

People think that *changing* is the risk. Actually, the real risk is created by doing things without understanding *why* you are doing them.

"We always spend this money on catalogs, we always spend this money on TV advertising, we always sacrifice virgins on the full moon, we always beg at the table, we always have two ovens in our houses." With these viewpoints, you don't really understand if cause and effect and correlation between those things is real. They *might* be. But companies, organizations and individuals rarely question that position. As a result, they often do things that may have no effect at all.

Excession Events switch this linear, status quo business model from one of ineffectiveness to one of real danger.

Einstein once said, "To do the same thing and expect a different result is the definition of insanity." Because of Excession Events, the success that you are aiming for—the result that you seek—changes. In some cases, it may be constantly changing. Therefore, to do the same thing and expect a completely different result becomes madness.

It's bad enough for a business to base its actions on reasons that are no longer relevant; that are long lost in history. It's even worse to continue with these actions, expecting them to deliver different outcomes.

If an organization, for example, is in a market where the average sales price of its product drops by a factor of 10 in three years, to continue to have a business model that is predicated on expensive salespeople going off to see individual clients becomes the wrong answer. Most companies will simply try and make the existing business model fit a new paradigm anyway. This approach absolutely fails. You might get away with it for a little while, but when an Excession Event brings drastic change, you'll never be able to adapt if you keep your model the same.

Our earlier chapter on Blockbuster exemplifies this. When change started affecting Blockbuster, they could have said, "Right, well, we're not making as much money as we did, so the thing we need to do is open more stores." Opening more stores might actually bring you in a bit more revenue in the short term. But long term, it is a catastrophic strategy! Because now you're signed up for leases in buildings, you've got bigger staff costs, you've got larger investments. Plus, people now want digital delivery, not brick-and-mortar. As the outdated business model starts to crater, you actually crash quicker because you've invested in the wrong direction.

If we believed the sun went around the Earth, it wouldn't do much harm on our day-to-day lives, but it'd be very important when we decide to launch satellites. Our knowledge tells us what we know. We see the world in a certain way because we are in a certain position.

It reminds me of the story of the blind monks patting the elephant. One of them has got a trunk, one has a leg, one has an ear, and one has the tail. If they don't speak to each other, then they all think that what they're touching is something entirely different from everybody else because they've never experienced an elephant before.

If you're holding the tail, well, you're going to think of the thing as a very different experience than others will, and therefore the assumptions you make about it are very different from somebody who's holding the trunk, the ear, or the leg. What this means is that your view of the universe is partial at best.

* * *

If you had Aristotle's view of how the universe works, you

could never create gunnery tables. Aristotle's logic said that if you fire a cannon, the cannonball goes in a straight line and then it just drops vertically. Aristotle knew nothing of parabolas; he didn't believe they existed. And it didn't matter to him because he lived over 2000 years before cannon fire became an issue for anyone. So if you're a 15th century cannon maker or cannon user and you use Aristotle's logic when you're aiming at the enemy, you're going to lose every battle because you can't work out how to hit anything.

This example is important because it underscores that knowing *how* to think can give you a great advantage over simply possessing knowledge.

Two people might have exactly the same knowledge of technology—in this case, a cannon—but might think about the cannon in different ways. The guy with the more modern understanding of parabolas is much more likely to kill you with his cannon than the guy who is using Aristotle's outdated concepts of how cannonballs travel.

The universe changed with the advent of the cannon. Until then, nobody cared about parabolas. Then, quite suddenly, parabolas and gunnery artillery tables were not just brought to existence, but immediately made important: A matter of life and death.

If someone thinks in a different way, then they are capable of coming up with a whole bunch of new ideas. If you use old ways of thinking, then you're never going to get to a new way of doing things because you're never going to consider that it would even work.

For example, how could you come up with the mathematics for a satellite if you thought that the sun went around the Earth? You'd be concerned that you'd hit the moon because, after all, it's on a glass sphere above the Earth, not very far away. None of your math would work; it would all go haywire.

As soon as you think differently, then what you can imagine changes.

GAMBLERS, STOCK BROKERS, MICHAEL CAINE & DOC HOLIDAY

Why do we hate change? It's simply human nature, and they've proven this time again. Part of the reason why change is so scary: The future is *always* risky.

In studies on people with gambling problems, for example, researchers would say to study subjects, "Let's make a wager. I'll toss a coin, and if it's heads, I'll give you $1,000. But if it's tails, you give me $500." People won't do it. They are more concerned with losing what they have than the potential gain, however good that gain is, because the future is unknown. As a result, they have a predilection for maintaining the status quo.

Research has also shown that when stock brokers have relatively little money—which, for them, is between zero and $5,000,000 of personal wealth—then they are quite laissez-faire. They will go for it and take risks because they've got very little to lose. These people are very aggressive and often highly successful.

Then, once they're between $5,000,000 and $15,000,000 net worth, they become very conservative because they *almost* have enough that they'll never need to work again. Losing it would be catastrophic.

The third stage: Once they get over about $15,000,000

worth of personal wealth, they're working on the principle that, "I could finish tomorrow and it doesn't matter because I've got so much money that I'll live well for the rest of my life." Therefore, they become highly aggressive and happy to take risks again.

Very few people in our society are in the "big bet" business where they are personally worth over $5,000,000. As a result, most people are far more nervous of losing what they have today than any potential upside that is unknown. So, what I have today is worth far more to me, psychologically, than some potential upside in the future.

The other problem with the future/the past is you can see this linear growth, but you can't see what the future Excession Event could be. As a result, you don't know that it might not ruin you. So, people are quite rightly somewhat nervous of the future.

Michael Caine was once asked how he picked what movies he would be in. Though he's picked some great scripts, Michael Caine is also notorious for picking some truly awful movies to be in. Answering the question, Caine said, "One, acting is my work and if someone offers me work, I take it." When the follow-up question asked, "Well, how do you pick which particular pieces you do?" Caine replied, "Someone sends me a script, I read the first page and the last page. If I've got dialogue on both the first page and the last page, I take the job."

People psychologically want that to be true. They don't want the idea that, "I've invested in the present and if the future changes, well, what about all the investment I've already made? I may not be in the position that I'm in now."

The funny thing is that very few people are at the absolute bottom. If you're at the absolute bottom of a society, you've got nothing to lose. It's the Doc Holliday problem.

Doc Holliday was the best, most efficient gunslinger in the West for a number of years. The reason why is because he was dying of tuberculosis, and he knew it. He didn't care less what happened to him because he was dying anyway. He would pull the gun before the gunfight even started and shoot people. He'd shoot them in the back walking out of the saloon; he'd do whatever it took because he was a man who had nothing left to lose. Very few people in our society are in that position and, as a result, they become risk-averse.

This is one of the reasons why you see people like Elon Musk or Richard Branson can make wild business decisions. They know that the safety net for them is very high, very strong, and two inches below them. If Branson's airlines all go bust tomorrow, he can go back to Necker Island and he can sit there and look out at the Caribbean for the rest of his life and go, "Well, it's a shame about the airline, but hey, I'm fine."

For most of us, the safety net is nailed to the floor. If you don't have a safety net, you're going to be much more risk-averse. It's 100% certain that you were alive until yesterday, even now, but I can't guarantee that you'll be alive in 24 hours from now. The future is always risky.

FIVE

The Escher Dilemma

Our instinct to make order of data—in the same way we do when we look at an optical illusion—reinforces our unconscious biases.

Human beings are pattern machines. We see faces in everything. You look at an electrical socket or :-) and the face will emerge. The classic duck-rabbit illusion exemplifies this further. Take a look:

Both of the images you see are true, and neither of them are true. At any moment you can see one but not the other. The reason for this is because it is genetically built into us to see faces and to see patterns, even when there aren't any. I'll explain why.

Imagine you're walking across the savanna and, through the grass, you see the face of a lion. You go, "Oh my, there's a lion." You run away. If there wasn't a lion and you just imagined it, then you've got a bit sweaty, you've burned a few more calories, and you're still alive. You can then pass on your genes to the next generation. All because you recognized the pattern of a lion and fled.

If, however, you're walking across the savanna and you think you see a lion and go, "Nah, there's no lion there, I was fooled," and then there *was* a lion...well, you've just removed yourself from the gene pool.

Human beings are pattern machines. We have a built-in propensity to see patterns because it's a great survival instinct, even when there isn't any real threat. The problem with that is that we end up failing to understand the difference in business between causation and correlation.

We correlate these things all the time. So, as pattern machines, we see the smiles in the jungle or the lions in the savanna because it's built into us to do it. It is what it is, but we've got to be aware that that happens. We've got to stop letting our inner caveman voices make all the decisions for us. We are rational machines that can get past that early programming if we choose to, but we have to make a conscious effort to do so.

Take a look at the image below.

It's an image that makes perfect sense as a 2D image, but your brain tries to see it in 3D, and it's confusing. You look at it and your brain makes sense of something that isn't there; it isn't true. So, even when there's no information, your brain will see a pattern anyway.

The problem with seeing the pattern is that the brain then starts making assumptions. It acts on things that aren't there. Even when you know there's nothing, or that it just doesn't make sense—like the diagram—you still see it.

We all have this built-in propensity to see patterns, to make sense of the data, and then to act on that data. The problem with this pattern recognition issue is that we end up making an assumption of a certain position. We then look for data that fulfills that position. You make sense of it, whether it's real or not, because the caveman part of your brain tells you to. As a result, you end up doing *correlated* ideas rather than *causation* ideas.

Here's an example: "I always rub my lucky rabbit's foot before I get on the football field."

"Why?"

"Well, because if I don't, I don't play well."

Of course, there is no evidence to suggest that the rabbit's foot is the cause. If you lose, it's got nothing to do with the rabbit's foot. It's got everything to do with the way *you* work.

We end up doing, personally and in business, many things that really don't make any sense. But we keep doing them because we've always done them. We never question it, we just keep making sense of the data. This is even *truer* if the data is confirming your existing prejudices.

Our dear MBA culture embodies this perfectly. As we've established, the MBA tells you what to think. It hard-wires your brain into believing. If you spent a few hundred thousand dollars on a Wharton MBA, they will teach you, "Look at this picture, and find the duck. There's a duck in this picture." Of course, you will see the duck.

But if you go elsewhere and they instruct you to look for the rabbit, you probably won't look for alternatives. You'll see the rabbit. The MBA does that. It tells you, "This is the pattern you're going to be looking for," and then you see those patterns. What the MBA *doesn't* say, is, "Oh, and by the way, there might be other things."

The MBA never looks for alternatives. It's like being in a room with a whole bunch of distinguished colleagues, and somebody says, "Here's a picture of a duck," and everybody agrees. Nobody in that instance wants to go, "Actually it's a rabbit." Because who wants to be that guy?

* * *

Ludwig Wittgenstein, the fairly famous Austrian philosopher and scourge of teachers around the world, was once asked by one of his students, "Why were those people in the Middle Ages so stupid that every morning they watched the dawn and thought that the sun is going around the Earth, when we know it's the exact opposite?" He replied, "Yeah, but what would it have looked like if it had been the other way around?" Of course the point is it would have looked exactly the same.

What you know today defines what you see. One of the things that Excession Events do is to *change* what you see.

In order to anticipate Excession Events, what you and I and all of us must equally and continuously do is question our existing assumptions. That is something that most of us do not do. Things like higher education, MBAs, the way that business is organized today—it ossifies our thinking. We cannot think about new and upcoming problems because we don't even perceive them to be problems.

For a few thousand years, people thought that the sun went around the Earth. That was fine because, one, everyone else thought it; two, saying otherwise would get you burnt at the stake because you became a heretic to the Church; and thirdly, it didn't make any difference whether you thought that or not; it was irrelevant.

The only time it mattered whether the Earth went around the sun or the sun went around the Earth was after we decided to start launching satellites. Then, it made a big difference.

TOLSTOY AND THE DOWNSIDE OF "INTELLIGENCE"

"The most sophisticated of ideas can be communicated to the simplest of men if before you tell them the answer they have no idea what the right answer is. But the simplest of ideas cannot be understood by the most intelligent of men if before you tell them the answer they have already made up their mind what the correct answer is."

— TOLSTOY

To manage Excession Events, you must be the person who doesn't know. Having an attitude of, "I know the answers," is a problem—partly because of the half-life of facts, and partly because knowing the answers means you're not open to new positions. You become dogmatic.

To avoid this, what all of us must do on a continual basis is be the simplest of men. Because if we're not, then we're going to end up in a position where we think we know. Then, that brings us back to Jefferson, who said, "A man who knows nothing is closer to the truth than a man whose mind is full of lies and half-truths."

SIX

The Elvis Impersonator

As pattern recognition machines, we humans tend to extrapolate in ways that don't make sense. We will extrapolate to the infinite. A perfect example of this is that *Mad Magazine* back in 1977 estimated there were 170 Elvis impersonators around the world. By the year 2000, it was estimated that there were about 85,000 Elvis impersonators in the world. So if you were to extrapolate *that* out, by the year 2043, everyone on the planet would be an Elvis impersonator.

Now we all look at this and say, "That's absurd." But plenty of people will take the business model of an organization, like Ford or Microsoft or Apple or any other number of businesses, and they will extrapolate that out to way beyond the point where it makes any sense.

Let's say I'm a CEO of a company, and my organization's stock shares are predicated on the future, not the present (that's all of them). Someone asks, "What's the future for your business

95

look like?" If I turn around and say, "Well, five years from now I've got no idea what business we're in." Even if that's true, and it often is, if you were to say that, you probably wouldn't even make it back to your office before you'd been fired.

Small businesses don't have quite so much pressure on them. But midsize to larger organizations have shareholders, they have pension funds, they have banks who offer credit, they have a whole set of institutions built around them that are specifically designed around linear growth for that organization. If you say anything other than, "Our growth is linear," then you scare them, because they are more frightened of the future than they are of the past. So to cope with this, we extrapolate to some absurd infinite. It could be six months from now, it could be 20 years from now. As long as there is a linear projection, people feel secure.

Oil companies and oil economies are a perfect example of this type of linear extrapolation. They all made assumptions around oil price being $100 a barrel. The Russian economy or the Venezuelan economy is predicated on that. But now it's $50 a barrel. Who can tell that it's not going to be $22 next month, or $150 next month? This lack of predictability causes enormous stresses in an organization, and ultimately, in a system.

So what can you possibly do about it? It's a problem for not just the oil companies, but for many organizations. I'm not blaming them for wanting a predictable future. But to just blindly believe that things grow in linear ways is a very short-term concept that paradoxically creates considerably more risk.

The trouble with extrapolating into the infinite is it leads into the most deadly human thinking, which is, "If you always do what you've always done, you'll always get what you've always had."

Many people would take the certainty of the present than the potential of an upside in the future. "I'm doing okay now, that's great. Therefore I will continue to do this and I know that I'll die quietly in my bed at the age of 102. That's fine with me."

Of course, this doesn't happen because we cannot control the world around us. Other people's Excession Events, which are far beyond our control, can overwhelm us when we're minding our own business. These Excession Events and other unpredictable occurrences make it too difficult to find a winning formula and simply stick with it. You need to be adaptable enough to change with the environment.

Adaptability means that you need to be more like Intel as an organization. From the outside, Intel looks very stable because it just simply follows Moore's Law: Every 24 months it produces twice the processing power. At a macro level, it has achieved enormous stability over the last 30 years or so. However, on the inside, Intel is constantly reinventing. There's no one magic formula that gives you Moore's Law; it's hundreds of small inventions that, added together, give you a result. Organizations need to understand that lots and lots of little things added together can produce enormous changes.

Now what Intel hasn't yet managed is a true Excession Event. They've just been extraordinarily successful at the linear way of doing business. One could argue that perhaps Moore's Law has actually held them back, because it's defining what they *think* their future looks like. Having said that, the myriad small decisions they make every day are helping them keep up with a very impressive linear growth.

One of the "little" things that Intel did, as an example, was to invest. Intel has processors built on silicon architecture, but there is another material that chips can be made out of called gallium arsenide. Now, gallium arsenide has certain advantages over silicon, as well as certain disadvantages. Intel has never made a gallium arsenide chip, at least not yet.

Some have suggested that gallium arsenide chips could overtake silicon chips—which led to rumblings that Intel could be put out of business by gallium arsenide processors built by somebody else.

The interesting point here is that Intel has actually invested hundreds of millions of dollars in gallium arsenide companies over the last 20 years. They acknowledged the possibility that they could be Excession Event-ed to oblivion by another technology, and so they hedged their bets. They didn't build gallium arsenide technology themselves, but they invested in organizations that *did*.

The end result was that gallium arsenide wasn't the right answer. Sure, Intel spent some money to find that out, but it was a useful investment that brought them valuable knowledge. More importantly, Intel's gallium arsenide saga shows their adaptability: They paid attention, acknowledged a potential Excession Event on their horizon, and planned accordingly. If Intel had just blindly extrapolated a linear future, gallium arsenide would have held the potential to destroy their entire organization.

* * *

The ability to adapt to Excession Events is more important now than at any other point in history. We established earlier that Excession Events are happening with increasing frequency, but that is just part of the picture. The bigger difference now is that, because of today's technology, Metcalfe's Law and Moore's Law, the steps between one change and the next are enormous—and getting bigger all the time.

In today's climate of drastic change, to be even a *single step behind* could mean complete catastrophe.

The film *Captain Phillips* illustrates this beautifully. In the film, Somali pirates face off against Navy SEALs. The SEALs' technological advantage over the Somali pirates was so enormous that the pirates couldn't even comprehend what was going on.

The Navy SEALs had radar, they had drones, they had all the

technological heft behind them that allowed them to identify the Somali pirates, know who their families were, know what their background was, know what weapons they had, and know what they were after. They knew *everything* about these people. They could even sit there and listen to the conversations that were happening in the lifeboat because they had special microphones that could penetrate its hull.

The Somali pirates were so completely lost, it was like a space alien turning up and meeting a caveman. There was just no common ground at all. And that was just a *few* generations of technological changes between those two groups!

The step changes are becoming bigger. They double every 24 months. Or, if you prefer, the step changes undergo an X-squared growth chart that Metcalfe's Law gives us. This means that the step change between the technological difference now and one in another two years from now could be as big as all the other changes previously *combined*—because we're going up by an X-squared rate.

Today's accelerated change that's occurring in bigger steps each time presents major challenges. The step change difference in the next generation could be so big, that being left behind by a single generation could be disastrous. You just couldn't keep up. But with the right mindset, you can manage even the biggest step change.

Remember Tolstoy's observation that you don't need to be the most intelligent of men to understand change and cope with a new world order? It seems that it's a positive *disadvantage* to be one of the intelligent men. What you need is to simply be open-minded. As long as you're prepared to sit and listen to the new facts as they occur, take them at face value, and then make decisions that aren't predicated on old thinking, old ideas, or old facts, then you have an ability to keep up.

But if you go into a problem knowing answers, believing facts, and not questioning existing assumptions, then you're going to be in serious trouble.

PART THREE

In the Land of the Blind

SEVEN

Think Long Term

In 1996, Apple was in dire straits. Apple was in so much trouble that Michael Dell stated that they should simply close down and return their shareholders' money. Today that sounds absurd, but at the time it seemed like an entirely logical thing to do. Part of the problem was that Apple had a wide range of products, and was trying to be all things to all people.

This all changed when Steve Jobs came back. Upon his return, Jobs told his senior staff, "This is a $9 billion business today. You need to come back to me with a plan to make this company profitable at $5.2 billion dollars annual revenue, and you need to do it in two weeks."

It was a shocking state of affairs, but of course Jobs was right. What Jobs realized more than anyone else in the IT industry, was that Apple's linear business model was failing. They were effectively managing decline. Keep in mind, this was a $9 billion dollar business; not what most people would class as a company that was about to go bust.

Steve Jobs realized that if they were to pivot the business, they couldn't do it with the existing linear mindset. Instead, Jobs decided Apple had to lighten the boat. They tossed a lot of products that didn't have a future overboard—even though many of these products were making money in the short-term. The advantage was, and Jobs recognized this: A lighter boat is an awful lot easier to steer.

Jobs was able to do this pivot because he couldn't care less what the market thought of him. Imagine if Jobs had gone to the stock market and said, "I'd like to change Apple completely in a totally radical way, and go in a direction no one has ever gone before." If he had to borrow money to do that, the chances are he wouldn't have gotten a dime. The financial institutions, shareholders, pension funds and other stake holders that run these businesses would have simply said "no."

To these groups, it might have seemed Jobs' new direction for Apple was moving backwards. But in reality, the ability to move backwards in the short-term is crucial for long-term gains. By streamlining, Jobs pivoted Apple to a new way of doing business. As the results can ably demonstrate, it was an extraordinarily successful turnaround.

Jobs understood that every change in business has an accompanying "dip." When a business needs to pivot to a new business model, what many companies don't seem to understand is that there will be a time in which revenues will drop. This is the dip. During this restructuring process, change may need to be radical in order to succeed. Companies need to be prepared to weather that storm for a long period of time.

A protracted amount of time in the modern era is no more than three months because that's what the stock market typically gives you. If Steve Jobs had been a slave to shareholders, he would have only been able to make changes that could have been implemented in three months.

The reality is that transforming your life or business takes time, and it's important to have a long term view in order to find the best path. To achieve this, you need very strong management that's open to new ideas and has good vision. Most importantly, you need to have bravery to get through that challenge—like Steve Jobs.

Unfortunately, a lot of companies would rather manage their existing business rather than radically change it. They would rather go for a safe 10% increase than the more extreme change that might yield a 10x increase.

A perfect example of that would be when IBM sold their hardware business. They could have done what Apple did and *changed* their hardware business, but they decided the best thing to do was to sell it to somebody else. Now, Lenovo owns the IBM PC and low end server hardware business. Similarly, Sony, at the time of this writing, is in the process of selling off its Vaio business.

Most organizations are like IBM and Sony in this regard: They are simply not prepared to go through big pains. They'd rather give it to somebody else to do. Often, it's easier for the new guy to come in and fire two-thirds of the staff, because they don't know them, and then start the business afresh. That's the sort of radical thinking that organizations need to be able to cope with, rather than simply staying the course with what they have today.

Had Steve Jobs done what shareholders wanted, Apple would not be the dominant force it is today. This is one of the biggest problems for most businesses today, particularly in the U.S.: They are beholden to the stock market. Even if they're not in the stock market today, they act as if they are because they want to look attractive to the kind of organizations that either are in the stock market and might want to buy them. Or, they want to look like a stock market listed organization so that when they *do* list on the stock market, they will have data that shows they were successful in the past, and fit within a certain set of criteria.

As a result of the obligations to shareholders, organizations often can only propose change that can be implemented in three months. Organizations want to pivot very quickly, but they don't want to go through the subsequent "dip" that we discussed earlier. The fact of the matter is, during a pivot, they're going to lose some speed, they're going to lose revenue, and they're not going to be able to keep up a market share.

Many of these big organizations seem to believe that through some strange force of will, or from some CEO's magical management decision, they can pivot and create a dramatic change in a short period of time without making any sacrifices. This is what I call "magical thinking," and it gets in the way of real progress. Instead, it's important to have a long term view in order to find the best path there.

You can't go through an Excession Event without going backwards at some level. It's one step back to take two steps forward.

*　*　*

Another aspect of magical thinking in business is that many organizations like the idea of *not* having competition in a market; but actually, to have a competitor makes it a market. If there are two players, it proves that a market exists. You might not even have to be first in the market to have the upper hand over your competition, either. A strong argument can also be made that, for many organizations, being the fast follower can be just as good, if not better, than being the first guy to do it.

You can take advantage of being a "fast follower" if you keep your mind open to new ways of thinking. Somebody else may have invented a new way of thinking, but you can *perfect* it. It's a perfectly reasonable sentiment that if you see the bandwagon, it's already too late. But if you're ready and brave enough to make the decision to fast follow somebody else into a market, it actually can be a real advantage.

To grasp how this works, imagine bicycle racers on a velodrome. If there are two guys on the track, the second guy gets the draft of the first. So, the strategy is that two cyclists will cycle as slow as they can for most of the race until it's about 200 meters to go and they'll stand on the pedals and they'll not go anywhere. Then finally, one of them will go for it. If he gets a half a second advantage over the other guy, he's going to win.

But if the second guy can grab his handlebars, hang on and pedal hard as he can as soon as the first guy goes, and he's within a quarter of a second of the first guy doing it, then chances are that second guy will win. Why? Because he will be in the draft of the first guy, and that will save him 22% of his energy. At the last moment, he will have the energy to surge forward to victory.

Excession Events often don't make the first person a ton of money, but they can often make the second guy an absolute fortune. The innovator doesn't always win! It's a bit like a man running through a minefield: The first guy is going to lose a few limbs on the way through and may not make it, but he makes it a lot easier for the next guy, because at least he knows where not to go.

Of course, even if you are the victor of the bike race, even if you make it through the minefield, all wins are temporary. You need to constantly be looking for the guy who's about to spring away and be on his wheel. When you see him, you can either decide to be the first guy to go, or you can be the fast follower.

But if you vacillate—if you decide to sit back and wait to see what happens—then you've already lost. You'll never be able to keep up. And as we've discussed, as markets accelerate, we have less and less time to decide whether or not to jump into the race. If you're a millisecond too late, you'll be left behind forever.

* * *

In this chapter, we've talked about how organizations will often stick their heads in the sand when confronted with things they don't want to acknowledge. Taking a step backwards to move two ahead? No. Competition? Doesn't exist. Excession Event on the horizon? Nope. The future? Well, that will be just like the past was, only *better*.

Just because organizations *believe* something to be true (or believe something doesn't exist) doesn't make it so. Unfortunately, so many organizations get so wrapped up in their product or themselves, they fail to understand that *what they think doesn't matter*. It's what the *market* wants that matters. If the market doesn't want what you have, you're not going to be able to defy gravity for any period of time.

In business, it is impossible to say, "We'll be linear for five years, and then there will be an Excession Event which will change the company, but in every way it will be a positive thing. Then we will zoom away in another linear for some period of time, until the next Excession Event, then we will do it again."

An organization might *believe* this will happen, but the world simply doesn't work that way. What success looked like in a market for the user of your product can and will change. In addition, what success looks like within the organization itself can change.

For example, if Kodak had said, "We're going to move directly and only into the digital camera market," they could have owned the digital camera market. However, they would be an entirely different and much smaller organization than they were during the film days, because the whole market for digital photography was tiny when it started out, relative to the market for film cameras.

Kodak could have conquered the digital photography market without actually being anything like the organization they were before. By one definition they would have won; they'd have dominated a massive market. By another definition, they would have lost; they would have taken several steps back in the short term. It depends on your definition of "winning."

In the face of Excession Events, your definition of winning needs to change, just as the market changes its definition of what is successful.

* * *

When companies play it safe, they avoid big changes. They will look at short term gains only, and will often come up with 10% increases like "working harder" or "optimizing." This conservative approach stops real thinking. When companies are willing to explore the possibility of moving backwards, of embracing changes, they can then open up options that wouldn't otherwise exist, and might even be the best long term path.

Of course, there is a side effect of leaving the status quo. When companies decide to go for a 10× solution like Steve Jobs did, they undertake massive risk. But businesses must to do this: They must make a conscious decision to place a bet on the future. They can either continue in a linear way and hope that somebody else doesn't come and reinvent them, or they can reinvent the market themselves. If they can do the latter, they have a chance of winning the lion's share of a new market.

If you are willing to reimagine everything and climb down one ladder, you may create an opportunity to climb a taller ladder and realize 10× gains.

EIGHT

Know Your Customer

Throughout this book we've talked about how Excession Events are technologies coming together to allow people to build something new that revolutionizes the way people think about what success is. However, just like emerging technologies, business models can be Excession Events, too.

It could be argued that business processes can be bigger, more efficient and more effective Excession Events than technological changes. Southwest Airlines is a great example of how a business model can create a tidal wave of change.

Southwest Airlines, like many airlines, started as a small carrier. They were based in Texas, out of Dallas Love Field. They began flying around Texas and they did reasonably well. They grew, but not in the same way that United and American and the other big players did. Instead, Southwest did a couple of things very differently.

The first thing they did was to always buy the same airplane. This gave them efficiency of scale; maintenance was easier, and they could turn the aircraft around in a much more efficient way than other suppliers. It also didn't matter which plane was in what location. They were all the same. This made them less fragile and even *more* efficient.

Southwest also realized that their competition was not other airlines, it was the Greyhound bus. And so, Southwest made the flying experience relatively sparse: They didn't offer food, there was no first class, and they got away from assigned seating.

Instead, Southwest offered "open" seating. They made their tickets extremely inexpensive, so every airline seat was full on every flight. And they realized that if they turned the aircraft around, they could sweat this extremely expensive asset far more efficiently than all the other suppliers could.

Unlike United, American or the other big airlines who made their money out of business class users, Southwest realized they would rather make a little money out of a lot of people. This gave them a major advantage, particularly for regional flights where the number of personal trips was likely to be higher than business users. The business users were more difficult to get to swap to Southwest initially, as they were already wedded to the loyalty schemes of the big players.

With the 737 aircraft Southwest used, there was no need to have hub-and-spoke-type airline systems. These systems are where the big players have large aircraft that fly between their hubs, and then small aircraft that fly between their hubs and the final destination of the client. Southwest changed these rules. They simply said, "We will fly direct." If you lived in cities such as Austin and San Antonio, where previously every flight basically predicated you going through Dallas or Houston, Southwest now allowed you to fly directly. They opened these direct flights to a whole range of additional destinations, too, making life much easier for travelers.

So by sweating assets harder, filling the airplanes, and competing with a different market (Greyhound), Southwest built themselves a great customer base. What Southwest realized next was that being nice to your clients doesn't cost any money. They started placing an emphasis on being sincere with their clients. They conveyed that they cared for customers and wanted their business. Meanwhile, the traditional airlines continued treating anyone other than first-class passengers like scum.

Everyone always used to complain about the big airlines, because they all played the same game. There really wasn't any other option for flying, so the big boys could get away with this. But of course, as soon as Southwest started being nice to their customers, which they were from the very start, then people started seeking out Southwest—even though they didn't get a first class seat or the nice upholstery.

What Southwest flyers *did* get was an opportunity to travel for a reasonable cost. There were a lot of direct flights so fliers got to their destinations faster and with less hassle.

They also got the feeling that Southwest, the company they were working with, genuinely liked them.

One of the things that's interesting to me about Southwest is that they spend an awful lot of their time talking to their staff about how to improve the experience for the passengers. The CEO of Southwest, Gary Kelly, has prided himself on spending weeks every year going to talk to all of the Southwest staff on a national basis and asking them how they could make the business better.

All of these steps deviated from the status quo, and all of these steps helped fuel Southwest's growth. Perhaps most importantly, as a result of these steps, Southwest has an extremely high customer satisfaction score *and* staff satisfaction score.

Other airlines and organizations would instead have people on the ground with great knowledge, and force them to work in a system that doesn't make sense. Why? Because some guy in senior management said so, or some focus group many years ago had decided that, "This is how we do the thing." In reality, the half-life of that fact almost certainly changed. Or, they may have simply built the process wrong in the first place. Either way, everyone was doomed to use the flawed system forever. This is terrible for morale and awful for business. These organizations refuse to reinvent the way that they do business, even after the facts change.

Southwest, on the other hand, was the "simple man." They ignored how other airlines worked. Instead, they asked questions. They listened carefully. As a result, they realized what success *really* was in the airline transportation market. They realized that every one of their customers mattered, not just the guys in the first three rows of the airplane. They realized that most people are more interested in getting there at a reasonable price than having a gin and tonic just before they take off. They realized that things like their rewards program shouldn't be a scam with draconian restrictions that are so complicated as to be unusable. Instead, Southwest implemented a flexible, generous rewards system that is easy to understand.

Southwest's rewards system is a perfect example of their genius. If you fly enough flights with Southwest, you get a Companion Pass. The Companion Pass means that any ticket you buy for the next 12 months, at any price, to go anywhere, you can take one named person with you. For the whole year.

This means that every businessman will hear this question from his partner before booking any business trip: "Are you flying Southwest?" Because his partner knows racking up the Southwest trips means that next year, they will get to join him on his journeys for free.

What Southwest has realized with this is that what benefits the spouse of the traveler is at least as powerful, and sometimes *more* powerful, than what that benefits the actual traveler. Very few people who fly the 1,000,000 miles a year that you need to get free flights are excited at the prospect of flying more. But if they get the opportunity to take their loved one on a vacation, with a free flight anywhere the airline goes, it produces an extraordinarily strong loyalty to the brand.

A perfect example of how *not* to run an airline would be United. In 2014, United had a bug in their computer system that enabled website visitors to get a first-class flight from London to the U.S. for $50. It was a major screw-up. Someone put it on social media, and a few thousand people bought $50 tickets. United Airlines then turned around and said, "Oh, no, no, no, that was a mistake, we screwed up. We're reneging on all these tickets," which of course angered the thousands who had bought them.

United's screw-up wasn't the computer bug. It was the missed opportunity. They could have turned a negative into a positive and directly built the most loyal set of 2,000 or 3,000 customers. They would have told their families and friends and everyone they ever spoke to for the rest of time. It would have been the best "accidental" word-of-mouth marketing initiative in history. But they threw it away.

Even worse than the lost opportunity was the damage United caused with their existing customer base. After voiding the $50 tickets, you had customers who were now thinking, "Now I can't go to that friend's wedding. Now I can't go to London for the weekend. I hate you, United." How much was that worth? United's poor decision-making in this instance is a clear example of how sticking to the status-quo perspective ("Free tickets after our mistake? We've never done that before, so we can't do it now.") can hold businesses back.

Now if Southwest Airlines had made a similar mistake, we know exactly what they would do, because their brand is so strong and consistent. Southwest would say, "We screwed up. Sorry about that. Have fun with the flights."

Southwest's way of thinking demonstrates quite nicely how a *business model* has the opportunity to be just as disruptive as any technological change. Southwest has no technological advantage over United or American or anyone else. They're not flying different aircraft; they don't go to different airports. They even serve the same crappy pretzels as everybody else. However, Southwest is a fundamentally different business.

* * *

After Southwest gained traction, other airlines, including EasyJet and Ryanair in Europe, tried to do a "fast follow." They looked at Southwest and thought, "No hubs, cheap airports, quick turnarounds, low cost...this means we can stuff the plane full of people very cheaply." They just assumed that people would fly with them if their tickets were cheap enough. That's great and it worked to a degree, but these airlines only learned *part* of the valuable lesson from Southwest.

At the time of writing Ryanair is making big efforts to improve its customer service. This will be interesting to watch.

What EasyJet, Ryanair and others missed was brand loyalty. They didn't offer any loyalty or frequent flier programs. They didn't smile at their passengers. They would rationalize that, because their tickets were cheap, it was acceptable to treat passengers like cattle. Customers would fly with them if their tickets were cheap, but as soon as a cheaper ticket was available they would bolt for that competitor.

Meanwhile, Southwest would say, "Because the ticket is cheap and the seats aren't very comfortable, we're going to be especially nice to you and it won't cost us any money." That, to me, is the killer avocation for Southwest. That's why they're an Excession Event as a brand, where so few others are.

* * *

All of this comes down to understanding your customers' motivation. Southwest understood that their competition was never going to be United or American or Delta or any other big airline. They realized that their customers' motivation was to get conveniently and quickly and inexpensively to another city—that's why so many of them were taking Greyhound buses. So instead of trying to copy the big airlines in the bustling airports, Southwest set up shop in smaller airports and flew direct. This perfectly addressed the motivations and needs of their Greyhound-grade customers.

If you want to position yourself to succeed through Excession Events, you have to understand what business you are *really* in. Southwest knew from day one that they were in the "people transportation" business. It just happens that the vehicle they use to transport you from one location to another is an aircraft...but I don't know that they would define themselves as an airline. They certainly don't think of themselves as a "Boeing 737 human cargo transportation organization."

On the other hand, when you look at United Airlines or American, they would say, "Our business is flying high-paying business and first class passengers from one location to another. Everyone else is simply the scum that pays for the fuel."

What far too many companies do is focus on themselves. They ask, "What's good for us?" What they should really be asking is, "What's good for the client?" Focus on what's good for your client and you find out what problem you're really solving. It's not always obvious. The answer that a client will give you, even if you ask them straight, is often hidden. But if you get the answer, and know what business you are in, you strengthen your defenses against unpredictable events.

* * *

If we could ask my great-grandparents what business they were in, they might say "the cart business." But in reality, they were in the finance business, because of the way their clients would rent carts from them. They had relationships with these people; they knew they paid their bills. This is in a time before credit rating agencies or any ability to take a credit history of someone. Now, if they had started selling these people trucks rather than renting them hand-pulled or horse-pulled carts, then they probably could have moved into the automobile world fairly seamlessly.

My great-grandparents also could have answered, "Well, actually we make wheels, but we're good with wood." So perhaps they could move themselves into the *woodworking* business. Or, they could have said, "We're in the business of wooden wheels, it's going away, but nobody else has noticed yet, but we noticed early so we'll sell the business and start again and do something else entirely." They could have bought 50 houses and built a real estate empire out of it. Hindsight is an exact science of course, but they certainly had options.

By understanding what business you're actually in, you can create options as to what you're going to do. My great-grandparents, unfortunately, opted to *not* make a decision. Instead, they continued thinking, "We're in the wheel business." They got that wrong. If you fail to recognize the business that you're *really* in, then it's not going to end well for you. It certainly didn't end well for my great-grandparents.

❊   ❊   ❊

Let's discuss Uber. What business is Uber in? Well, many people would say they're in the "unlicensed taxi business." That's actually pretty close to what they are: An unlicensed taxi business with a smartphone app attached. Interestingly enough, however, I think Uber has already realized that they're in the *transportation* business. They just presently need a driver at the front of the car to do their business. That too will change.

Recently Uber invested a large sum of money into Carnegie Mellon University to help them develop self-driving cars. As a result, they are now going to be, it appears, competing with Google and Apple, who are both rumored to be getting into the self-driving car business. At the time of writing this book, it's extremely difficult to imagine Uber and Google competing with each other—and yet, this now appears to be the case.

Since both of them want to be in the self-driving car business, and Uber has the transportation technology and process for moving people around, it seems likely that just the delivery mechanism will change. Google is in the self-driving car business because they understand mapping and the technology behind it. It will be interesting to see these how these two organizations, with entirely different cultures and outlooks, are going to mesh into a market or compete in a market. It is interesting to note that even as you see an Excession Event emerging, it is very hard to predict outcomes.

Uber's investment into Carnegie Mellon's self-driving car program is the kind of statement that gave them a $40,000,000,000 valuation. It's difficult to imagine how a taxi firm with an app could turn around and say, "We have a $40,000,000,000 valuation." But what people are doing, and it's questionable as to whether it's reasonable, is extrapolating two tiny numbers at the beginning of a graph and drawing out to infinity to come up with a number for Uber's valuation. That happens all the time, and whether it's reasonable is open to some significant debate. Of course, only time will tell.

Next up: What business is Netflix *really* in? Netflix has already changed their model a number of times, but they've never lost sight of the business they are really in: The entertainment business. First they delivered entertainment via DVD, then they delivered it via the Internet. Now, Netflix is creating its own original content, which is still under the "entertainment business" umbrella. Netflix is doing this because the advantage they had in streaming is beginning to be eroded by Amazon Prime Video, Hulu and Apple, as well as Sony and others.

With Netflix, what started out as a DVD delivery service is now a full-fledged production studio. It's pretty obvious that's where they're going. It will be interesting to see whether they even maintain their streaming division over time. Their next logical step is to attack the cable providers. All wins are temporary and the competitors are constantly changing.

* * *

If you want to know what business you're in, it helps to start asking questions like, "What problems am I really trying to solve?" and "How are customers actually using our product?" But to truly get to the bottom of things, you need to ask your *clients* what business *they* think you're in. Then, not only do you have to listen to lots of them and have an open mind, but you have to decide whether you want to take any notice of them.

The problem is that people hear what they want to hear. Instead, it's better to be the simple man. Be the man who doesn't know anything. Don't be the most educated of men. When you ask someone their opinion, and they start telling you something you don't like, don't argue with them. I've always found that funny, it's human nature. "So what's your opinion?" "Well, I think this." "Oh, no, you're wrong." "Hang on, you asked my opinion. Do you want it or not? I didn't say you have to take action on it."

I'm not saying that the thing to do is ask 100 of your customers what business you're in, and if 51 of them say you're in that business, then that's how you define yourself. You need to be in a position where you are at least open to the idea of seeing yourself in a different way. Asking your customers is a great way to do this.

I have personally found that I like to understand what motivates people because I can then predict their moves as a result of that. If I know a person is motivated in a certain way to do a certain thing, if I know that if I press a certain button with that person, then they will act in a predictable way. The thing I can't handle? People whose motivations I just don't understand. Their actions, as a result, become random. Random actions are no use. If actions cannot be predicted, then what's the point in interacting with them?

There is one group that I can predict quite easily, hence the following warning: When you try and find out what business you're truly in, do *not* ask the analysts of your existing business, the consultants in your existing business, or the suppliers in the existing business. They're all wedded to the status quo, and as a result they're not going to give you radical answers.

Also, when you ask someone, "Well, what should we do? What should we build?" Do not allow them to answer that without any consequences.

A past employer of mine went to a very large reseller of our technologies and said, "What do we need to do to get you to sell 1,000,000 of these things?" The reseller said, "You make it for $1,500, we'll sell 1,000,000 of them." *Really?*

So they assigned 50 engineers who spent two years building a $1,500 device. They showed it to the client who looked at it and went, "Well, what's that?" They said, "Oh, it's the $1,500 device you talked about two years ago." "Oh, did I? I don't remember that." That client wasn't invested in the answer. It's a bit like me sitting around and saying, "Oh, I want a car that looks like Chitty Chitty Bang Bang." As soon as it turns up, "Well, what the hell is that?" "You said you wanted this." "Did I? I don't remember that."

You've got to make certain that when you ask questions of a client, that client also understands that there is compromise in all these things. That changes the way that they talk to you. "I want a house that's small on the outside and big in the inside." "Well, I can't do that because it breaks the laws of physics." "All right, well, let's do something else."

You've got to keep clients within a tight set of bounds. Finding people who are good at asking questions, as this book discusses, is quite hard. People who are prepared to stand up to clients and internal people within the organization, and not be afraid to ask contrary questions...it's a dying breed, because asking those questions just might get you fired.

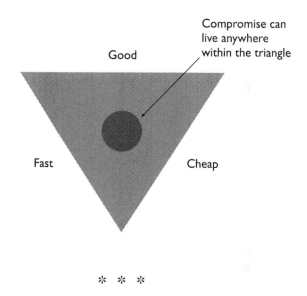

* * *

When you start asking questions about the nature of your business, the answers may seem obvious. Don't take these obvious answers at face value. Deeper examination often reveals they are not quite as obvious as they may seem.

Food is a good example of this. You can go to a range of different restaurants, but the true reason you choose one is not the obvious reason. It's not for the size of the portions. It's not that a more expensive restaurant will give you more calories than a cheaper restaurant. Often it's the other way around. Sometimes it's about flavor. I feel for many people it is about status; both to be seen with others and for the person that you're taking. If you take your new honey to Olive Garden, it's less likely to end well for you that evening than if you take them to a fancy steakhouse.

Many of the things we do in society are status-driven. That's not meant to make it sound like we're all shallow; it's just how human beings work. So restaurants, as a good example, often aren't about the foods—they're about how it makes you *feel*.

Another good example of that would be bejeweled Nokia phones. A jewel covered Nokia phone is no better than a regular Nokia phone, so why would you pay $20,000 for one? Well, what you don't do with a $20,000 phone is keep it in your pocket. It's all about status. That may sound very shallow but our society is largely driven by status.

No one ever bought a Rolex watch because it's a better time-piece than anyone else. I've got a Casio watch. It was $150, and it's tied to the atomic clock in Denver. It is accurate to one second every 1,000,000 years, but most people would say that a Rolex is better. But a Rolex isn't a watch—it's a piece of jewelry that tells the time.

This takes us back to understanding what business you're really in. Rolex know that they are in the jewelry business; they're in the luxury business. It just so happens the only reasonable socially accepted piece of jewelry a man can wear is a watch. For some reason our society has decided you can't have frivolous jewelry on men, unless you're a rapper. But if you're a businessman, you can't have a one-inch chunk necklace around your neck. You'd be laughed out the building. You *can* wear a $10,000 Rolex, but it's never about telling time. It's about telling people that you have arrived.

Johnnie Walker is another example of this. Japan is a big market for Scotch, and the Japanese have a perception that Scotch whiskey is the best whiskey in the world. Johnnie Walker sales were doing fairly well in Japan; however they started losing market share to some of the Japanese distillers because Japan also makes decent whiskey.

Johnnie Walker decided to lower its pricing. Normal price elasticity rules suggest if you lower the price, consumption will go up. It seems obvious enough, but it was a catastrophe for Johnny Walker. Their market share dropped precipitously. Then, they did some research and found out that people in Japan drink whiskey completely differently than people in Britain or America drink whiskey.

In Japan, business people take their bottle of whiskey to their bar. Often, if it's a bar they go to regularly, they leave the bottle there, and the staff will serve you your whiskey out of your bottle whenever you dine there. This means everyone gets to see what whiskey you're drinking.

In Japan, the more expensive the whiskey is, the higher status you are. And in a society such as Japan's, your status is critically important. So if you're drinking cheap whiskey, then you're not as high a status as the man who's drinking a high-status whiskey.

So when Johnny Walker dropped their price, it was a disaster because it showed that they were a "lower status" whiskey. Once they understood the market began producing Black, Green and Blue Label Johnnie Walkers. These 12-year, 18-year, and 24-year-old whiskies had big, colorful labels; someone 50 feet across the restaurant could identify you as high-status from your Johnnie Walker whiskey.

What Johnny Walker came to understand in Japan, as well as in other parts of the world, was their customers' motivation and also the business they are really in. The answers to both of these questions turned out to be *status*.

As a final word on the power of status, a few years ago there was a blind taste-off for about 100 different types of bottled and tap water from around the world. It was judged by aficionados of water. The third-place finisher was London tap water, easily beating out the many of the expensive waters, which cost $4.00 a liter. The representative from Thames Water stated that a bath full of London tap water, which is about 70 liters, would cost you about 25 cents. That proves the power of status.

✳   ✳   ✳

What business are you actually in? There's no clear answer to this question. But the important thing is to examine your assumptions, figure out what you're actually providing your customer, and make sure you're optimizing for that. You can't just do it once. Do it as an exercise. Always be testing.

In 2005, Tata Motors tried to build the world's first $1,000 car. It was a technically laudable thing to do. The trouble was that they didn't understand that the psychology of buying a car in India, which was their primary market, was all about status. It wasn't about whether it had four seats. People would put four people onto a moped anyway. It wasn't even about transportation; if they wanted a vehicle that transported stuff, they'd buy a tractor.

In India, a car is primarily about status: "I'm better than you because you ride a moped and I've got a Mercedes." But if my moped costs the same amount of money as your car, then your car has no extra status. You just look like a poor man because you have a cheap car.

This strategic failure was compounded by the fact the Tata caught fire a lot, which certainly didn't help. The Tata ultimately became a very cheap car that wasn't very cheap; it became a *non*-status symbol. Tata screwed up because they fundamentally failed to understand why anyone would by a car in India. They don't buy it for transport; they buy it to be *seen* in it.

NINE

Know Your Ecosystem

Frederick Tudor was an American businessman who sold ice in the 1830s. Ice is extremely useful for keeping things fresh, and food going bad was a major problem at that time. So Tudor started selling ice out of lakes that he would effectively "farm" in the Boston area. These lakes would freeze over in the winter. His people would go along and break up the ice with hammers and then they would sell it to stores in New York and Boston.

Around 1840, Tudor had an epiphany: People in the south would like ice, too. Nobody else was doing it down south, and it would be worth a lot more money. So he rented a ship, broke up a ton of ice, shoved it on the ship and shipped it down to Savannah, Georgia, and New Orleans, Louisiana.

When Tudor and his ice shipment arrived at the dockside, he found that 92% of the ice had melted. The ice that they did get off the ship they didn't know what to do with. Most of it melted on the dock because no one in New Orleans or Savannah had even seen ice before. The ice that did survive was put into the only place where you stored things and that was the salt house, where you would salt pork, beef and other meats. Of course, as soon as they put the ice in the salt it melted; that was that. It nearly bankrupted Tudor.

Within a few years, he was making his technology better. Instead of breaking up the ice, they started sawing it up out of the lakes, making ice blocks. These were far more efficient. Packed in saw dust, the ice blocks were ready to be delivered to ice houses ready to receive it. Ships for transporting the ice were well-insulated. They found if you used lots of sawdust and cut the ice into the right shapes to be stacked in the ship, they could keep it frozen a lot longer. They built an entire ecosystem around ice distribution.

By the 1870s, ice was going way beyond Savannah and New Orleans. There was a store in the Strand in London which kept a block of ice in the window. The ice was so pure and clear that they would hang a copy of the *Times Of London* behind it, and even though the block was three feet thick, it was possible to read the paper through it. The wealthy of London, the royalty and the aristocracy, would buy the ice from this store in London. That ice came from Boston.

By the 1890s, the ice was going even further afield. At the height of his business empire, Tudor was shipping ice as far as South Africa, Australia, Japan, and India. Ice in India was coming from Boston lakes.

All of this was because Tudor created an enormously efficient ecosystem. Now, Tudor was a strange character because he said that, of course, mankind could never make ice. After all, how would you come up with something that's colder than that, which would allow you to make ice? The interesting thing is, he knew that you *could* do refrigeration and you *could* make ice with a process that didn't involve "farming" it in nature. But Tudor suppressed this information.

Meanwhile, a doctor in Florida named John Gorrie believed his patients caught malaria because it was warm. It made sense: It was hot in Florida where everyone got malaria; it was cold in Boston where no one got malaria. His existing knowledge told him what to look for.

Seeking a solution to this problem, Gorrie worked out how to produce a vacuum pump. From a vacuum pump you can produce low pressure air. From low pressure air, energy was removed from the environment, causing the environment to cool. This produces cold, and from cold you can make ice. Gorrie invented his refrigeration technology in 1853, but Tudor kept him tied up in court for the whole of his career.

John Gorrie, who invented refrigeration, died penniless. Frederic Tudor, who crushed his idea, broke ice up and took it to Japan and Australia on ships, won. At least until others, whom Frederick Tudor could not crush, came up with the same refrigeration idea. Refrigeration in factories came out in the mid-1890s and none of the ice farming companies, including Frederick Tudor's, were able to survive the transition from ice distribution to ice manufacturing.

Then, none of those companies that had ice made in factories could transfer themselves into being organizations that sold refrigerators. We think of refrigerators as a 20th century device, but even until the '40s and '50s many people would have a block of ice delivered and have a cold cabinet rather than a refrigerator. This business was huge; in 1900 it was the ninth biggest business in America.

The point of the Ice King story is that just because you have a better technology, like Gorrie did, it doesn't necessarily mean that you're going to win. In some cases, the *ecosystem* becomes far more powerful than just the technology in its own right. Tudor's ecosystem was so well entrenched that he managed to put ice onto trains so that you could keep animal carcasses cool. Gorrie? He was just a man with an idea.

Let's recap the ecosystem that helped keep things cool. The first ecosystem for ice was the ice factories. Next was efficient electricity production from small coal-fired power stations. Once you had small power stations and the ability to produce electricity, then you make ice on site, wherever that happened to be. You no longer had to be near somewhere that was cold. Distribution became less of an issue.

The next step after the power stations was to give everyone the power of electricity into their own homes. Mass electrification from the early 1900s onwards allowed people and organizations to move away from having their own power stations. As a result, they simply plugged into the grid. This enabled them to harness power locally because, of course, you could simply plug into a wall.

These various ecosystems give us examples of how a number of technologies need to come together for certain things to happen. Someone could have, in theory at least, produced the refrigerator in the 1870s. But until the 1920s it was of no use because nobody had an electricity supply capable of running a refrigerator. The ecosystem has to be in place in order for some ideas to gain traction.

No person or business exists in isolation. We all depend on our surroundings, and are built on assumptions about our environment.

*   *   *

As we discussed earlier, the building blocks for a technology will come along, but they don't all come along at once. Once we get to the point where all of the pieces that are required for a technology to function are in place, then it spontaneously happens. This often occurs in multiple places simultaneously. We've already discussed this notion in the idea of pyramids; for refrigeration, there was certainly companies making refrigerators in numerous locations around the world and they all took off at the same time.

This didn't mean that refrigerators were universal. They were only universal where all this technology had coalesced. For example, in China there wasn't much in the way of refrigeration because there wasn't much in the way of electrification. China wasn't electrified until the 1960s. They were missing a key ingredient in the essential ecosystem, and so their refrigeration was delayed.

To be able to utilize a new paradigm shift, a new series of puzzle pieces have to be all clicked together. If we're personally not in a location where all of those pieces come together, then we won't be able to take advantage of that technology. But when the puzzle pieces are all present, it seems to be inevitable. Like a developing thunderstorm, when the right elements are placed in close proximity, there's really no stopping them from creating an *event*—including an Excession Event.

So if these events are inevitably going to happen, what can you do about them?

You can pay attention. If you're not aware that a number of pieces of technology are coalescing or are building on themselves, then you're going to get blindsided. You may only see three of the four elements or five of the nine elements. If you miss just one of them and you don't realize that 5G technology is coming, or there's been a breakthrough in battery technology, or processing performances have suddenly skyrocketed or any number of other pieces of the puzzle...if you can't see them all then you're not going to see the bigger picture. Simply paying attention is a critically important step to managing Excession Events.

Earlier we talked about the advantages of knowing less and less about more and more. To be a polymath: The person who sits above it all and has enough information about any one piece of the puzzle to see where it fits, without having to be an expert in any one piece. Because the trouble with being the expert is that it often means you need to have specialized, which takes you down the rabbit hole of not being able to see the bigger picture, and leaves you wedded and heavily invested in the status quo.

You must pay attention to surrounding areas too, as they may have an impact. For example, the car industry was blind-sided by the sort of technology that Elon Musk put together because he came out of a technology background. He knew all about things like laptop batteries and how, if you couple thousands of them together, they can give you a power plant that would enable you to have a high-performance and real-world usable electric vehicle.

Traditional car manufactures didn't know very much about electric batteries, and as a result, never even considered that it would be possible. It's absurd when you think about it: Elon Musk went from not even being in the car industry to having the best car in the world...in less than five years.

How did Ford, GM, Toyota, Honda, Hyundai, Bentley and every other car manufacturer on the planet totally fail to see the power of that? They failed to see it because they weren't in the technology business, and they weren't really paying attention. No one at Volkswagen or Toyota or anywhere else was noticing the growth in performance of laptop batteries. Meanwhile, I would argue that Musk's recognition of what could be achieved with batteries will be one of the single biggest technological breakthroughs in history.

Don't get me wrong; the electric motor is great, too. But anyone can make an electric motor of that quality. Musk's idea rendered big monolithic batteries obsolete. The notion that you could string together thousands of tiny laptop batteries was an absolute breakthrough. The rest of it was beautiful packaging. But Musk's thought process? It enabled him to do something no one else had considered.

* * *

The advent of the Tesla shows that venturing outside of your normal market and seeing that something that's entirely not in your world could replace your world completely.

The camera phone business is another good example. There is an old adage that says, "What's the best camera?" The answer, of course: "The one you've got with you." To solve this problem, camera manufacturers were trying to build better and better little compact cameras that were easier to carry. But in reality, these compact cameras were only useful if you had one with you all the time, which you probably didn't.

No one leaves the house without a phone. When Nokia, as an example, started putting cameras into phones, well, that should have been an enormous call to action for the camera manufacturers. But they were completely blindsided by it. They basically came up with the perspective of, "It doesn't matter because the picture quality of cameras on phones is not very good."

For that moment, it may have been true. But Moore's Law told you that within two to four generations, a mere three to seven years into the future, the camera phones would be 50 times better than they were at the beginning. As a result, camera phones would have the power to crush regular cameras because the processing power of that little supercomputer in your hand would enable everyone to produce photographs with such amazing quality, you couldn't possibly touch with a compact camera. Camera makers were not looking at their environment; they were not paying attention to these technologies. As a result, many were Excession Evented out of existence.

A lot of Excession Events, almost all of them, come from people who aren't wedded to the status quo within an existing environment.

Nikon and Canon were two camera companies who got into the compact camera space. It was a pretty diverse market, but these two companies were focusing on megapixels. "My camera is two mega pixels," one would say. "Well, ours is 3.2." "Well, mine has gone up to 5." While they were bickering and one-upping each other, they didn't even seem to notice that I have the same megapixel quality on my iPhone, and it's going to get even better. Plus, it has an intrinsic advantage over cameras: I'm already carrying it, practically all the time.

Nobody wants to carry two boxes. Even if it wasn't as good a quality picture, people were *still* more likely to use the iPhone than they were a small compact camera from someone like Canon or Nikon.

This changed what success looked like in a camera. Plenty of people have taken some horrible photographs with an iPhone. But that's okay because they're still better than the picture you *didn't* take with great camera that you haven't got with you.

The camera/phone event is especially fascinating because it illustrates how Excession Events can blindside business by coming from outside their industry. Nobody in the camera business was paying attention to phones. It was an entirely different industry. Even when the change arrived, a lot of people in the camera business believed that people bought their product because of the quality of the experience, the quality of the pictures it took. That may have been true, but the ecosystem changes that as well. Now, picture availability is more important than picture quality. The nature of viewing on screens, not print, also changes the quality dynamic. A far lower quality is required to display an acceptable image on screen than is needed for print purposes.

One of my sons has a digital SLR camera. Even though it takes beautiful pictures, he never uses it. He is simply not prepared to wait the few hours from the point where he took the picture to the point where he can actually get the picture on Instagram. He would rather take a worse picture and have it immediately available by having it on his iPhone than he would take a better picture with his SLR and then have to come home to upload it. For him, the SLR misses the spontaneity of the experience. The iPhone ecosystem is better because it can take a decent picture, but also upload it, put it on social media, email it, text message it, whatever.

This illustrates why real winners of many Excession Events are the people who either build it themselves or at least take control of the ecosystem. Then they make it profitable and advantageous for lots of other people to join in, whether they join in financially or they join in from a cultural or business point of view.

* * *

The modern container—as in the freight liner-type-container—was invented in 1956 after an ecosystem developed to sustain it. Of course, standardized containerization had been used in one form or the other since the 1850s. British coal miners were using containerization to transport coal out of the mines, put it on barges, and then onto ships to transport around the country and around the world. That was highly effective, but it was relatively small scale.

Containerization in the '60s changed shipping. It changed the world economy enormously. But it relied on a number of puzzle pieces coming together. They needed to be able to build a completely standardized and very accurately built steel container at a relatively low price. To achieve that, steel of a good quality needed to be available, as well as affordable manufacturing capabilities to build the containers. A single 20 foot container will cost you around $2000, by the way.

New large and powerful cranes needed to be developed to load and unload the new containers. Ships capable of carrying these containers needed to be built specifically for that purpose. To be cost-effective, they needed to be extremely large. As a consequence of this size requirement, they needed to have highly efficient diesel engines. You couldn't do this with coal; it wouldn't have been fast enough, it wouldn't be powerful enough, and it would take up too much room. As a result, you needed to wait until diesel engines were powerful, where you could install them in a very big ship.

Once the ships had been redesigned, harbors or container ports capable of coping with these enormous ships were required. Dredging harbors in order to accommodate the enormous ships was required. Lastly, infrastructure like the Suez and Panama Canals had to be of a capacity that they could cope with the size of all these ships.

If any one of those things had not existed, containerization could not have happened. Harder, stronger metals were the spark that kicked all this off. Without high quality, inexpensive steel none of this could happen. No containers, no large diesel engines, no huge steel ships. Research from the Second World War enabled all this to happen.

When containerization happened, it dramatically influenced business. As an example, Scotch whiskey used to leave Britain from ports in Glasgow and go to America. About 30% of it would "break" along the way. That was a high wastage level because, of course, all the dockworkers were stealing it. As a result, the amount of Scotch whiskey that needed to be sent to America to be sold was much higher than the amount that actually got there. This made the profit margins for the

Scotch whiskey manufacturers far lower than they wanted it to be, or than it really should have been.

After containerization, the stevedores (dock workers) working the docks didn't even know that the container had scotch whiskey in it. It was safely locked in a steel box. Nobody could get in. The wastage went from 30% to under 1%, vanishingly tiny. Containerization transformed Scotch whiskey in America; it became cost-effective to ship Scotch whiskey to the United States.

That's one of hundreds of examples of why containerization was important. And what did it ultimately allow us to do? It allowed the world economy to kick off globalization. Without containerization there would be no globalization because it simply wouldn't be cost effective to ship goods around the world.

That's a perfect example of a wonderful ecosystem; of how lots of different pieces of technology needed to come together for it to work. Once it did work, then everyone adopted it because it was an obvious thing to do. The next step after that was that it enabled lots of other people to benefit from the ecosystem. The guy who invented containerization benefited from it, but lots of other people did, too—from t-shirt manufacturers in China to Scotch whiskey distributors in Scotland.

It should also be noted that there were also losers in this transformation. In Britain, for example, Liverpool and London docks were devastated. Two of the largest ports in the world were not suited to containerization and thousands of jobs were lost as the ports moved away and mechanized. In London, at least many of the old warehouses are now extraordinarily expensive apartments. Liverpool has never recovered and continues to be a region blighted by poverty.

* * *

Around the year 2000, there was a plethora of companies that made MP3 players. Creative Labs was one example of a company that was actually making decent and relatively inexpensive MP3 players. Then Apple came along and changed everything with a brand-driven Excession Event: The iPod.

Apple launched the iPod in 2001. It had a 5 gig hard drive in it. It certainly was a larger capacity than everyone else's machine. Many people believe that the reason the iPod won was because of the large capacity. I would argue that the *real* reason Apple won was because of their ecosystem: iTunes.

When iTunes first came out, it had very few of the capabilities of the modern version, but it did have novel advancements for the time. If you put a CD into the side of your computer, iTunes had the capability to go visit the Internet, look up the meta data—the album liner notes and artwork—and download it to your computer. iTunes would organize all of your music, allow you to play it through your computer, and download the songs that you wanted to onto your iPod.

While there were many other mp3 players on the market,

none of them worked this way. None of them had an application that interacted neatly and seamlessly between the portable device that you listen to on the go and the device you listen to while at your desk.

Other mp3 players were *devices*, but they were not *systems*. Apple had created an extremely powerful ecosystem.

Apple then leveraged the ecosystem: They gave it away. Free iTunes for PCs helped sell more iPods, but more importantly, it allowed people to experience the Apple world. Those who weren't Apple customers were now seeing what a seamless experience the Apple world was—which the PC world was not, and still isn't. When that doorway was cracked open, people got a glimpse of the beautifully elegant way all Apple products interacted with each other, with iTunes as the "Gold Standard."

*　*　*

Invoking Victor Hugo once more, there is simply no stopping an idea whose time has come. When you then start stringing a series of ideas together and place them in the right ecosystem, you can achieve a multiplying effect. Of course, an idea can be an Excession Event without necessarily being an ecosystem. But an ecosystem can produce an enormously more powerful Excession Event.

The ultimate ecosystem may be life itself: There's abundant evidence that about 3.6 billion years ago, Earth was a churning mass of puzzle pieces that simply could not be stopped. They fit together to spark life. We have fossils to prove it. I do hope that we go and find life on Europa or Ganymede or some other moons of Jupiter or Saturn in the next few years. I have a strong suspicion it's going to look very similar to the life that we have on Earth—and that a similar type of ecosystem enabled it to happen.

TEN

Focus on the Questions, Not the Answers

We have established that groupthink and conformity can hold organizations back, and leave them highly vulnerable to Excession Events. Conversely, by building a contrarian company culture that encourages questioning and flexibility, you can promote growth and innovation—as well as an adaptability to help your organization thrive in times of change. Let's return to Netflix as a classic example of a healthy organizational mindset for growth and change.

Netflix did two turnarounds. Firstly, they went from a DVD distribution business to an online streaming business in 10 years. One of their big changes was to put their library online. People no longer needed to go to a store to pick up the movie. As soon as they didn't need to go to a store to rent the movie, and they could rent it online, then it seemed very logical that the next step would be to go from sending you the DVD to streaming the content. This massive leap of "I don't physically need to go anywhere to rent the movie" was a major Excession Event.

Secondly, Netflix has started writing their own media. They discovered they could be a studio, and not just the distribution company. Culturally, this was another Excession Event that may be at least as important as the first.

How did Netflix get there? They constantly re-examined who they were. They understood that they didn't know the answers. But they also understood that normal, average-standard levels of work are completely useless to them. Netflix is only interested in extraordinary talent and extraordinary thinking.

Netflix has a culture of being that's like a world class sports team. They only want the absolute best in the organization. They would rather get rid of standard players and enable the culture to have a hole in it, waiting for the next superstar to turn up. You're either the best there is or you don't work there. That is their culture.

The idea of being average is simply not good enough for Netflix. Even if you've worked there a long time and proven that you are extraordinary, you don't get tenure. It doesn't work that way. Netflix doesn't celebrate tenure. That doesn't mean that they want you to leave, but they don't regard a 10-year employee as "better" than a one-year employee.

As an aside, this "anti-tenure" philosophy is the opposite

of our education system, which is constructed around the very idea of tenure. You get more money for being there longer and you become bulletproof: You can't be fired. If that doesn't produce an ossified culture, then what does? You could argue that's one of the reasons our schools are doing so badly.

As an employee of Netflix, however, you never get to rest on your laurels. You constantly have to reprove yourself. If you show yourself incapable or unwilling to do that, then they will give you a generous severance package to go elsewhere. If you're not able to come up with new ideas all the time, they'll simply replace you with somebody who will. If you live in a culture where you know that's true, then you're going to either opt-out when you run out of ideas or you're going to strive even more to keep pushing the envelope. Netflix simply doesn't tolerate mediocrity. It must be a vibrant, if exhausting, environment.

Why do they have this stance? The answer may be in their own mission and their own documents, in which they say that the top players can produce 10x the result of second tier players. In a normal organization, second tier players would be entirely talented, decent, reasonable people. But Netflix needs *extraordinary* talent. Netflix's position could be regarded as a contrarian philosophy; it's certainly not how most other big companies work. Netflix is not interested in status quo 10% growth. They are fixated on the 10x leap.

Thomas Jefferson once said that every generation needs a revolution. I think that Netflix believes that, too. They seem to feel a need to keep the organization moving in a way that it never feels complacent. If it feels comfortable in a position, you're unlikely to move from it. Complacency is a killer of 10× results.

Blockbuster's complacency was that they thought they knew what the answer was: "People rent movies from stores." They didn't recognize that the DVD was simply a delivery mechanism. They probably loved the fact that people rented DVDs because they didn't wear out so fast, and they took up less room on the shelves than tapes. Blockbuster regarded themselves as being in the "DVD-renting business," and of course they were wrong.

Netflix could not have done what they did earlier. Even five years earlier it would have been impossible. For the Netflix model to work, their customers needed high speed internet connectivity, a low cost device to play the movies from, and inexpensive digital storage. None of these things were true. But once they all were true, then Netflix could exploit it.

It seems likely that Blockbuster had no contrarians and no extraordinary talent within the organization questioning their position at any time. Netflix did, and that's why they were able to understand the business they were *really* in: The "people watching films at home with their family" business.

* * *

Why doesn't business evolution, such as Netflix moving to

streaming, simply happen naturally? It may just be human nature. Institutions, by their nature, try to institutionalize everything. They try and say, "This is the way we do business. So therefore we will set up rules around how we do business that will never change."

Those rules are why you end up always cutting the ham in half. You end up with a culture within your organization that says, "We do this because we've always done it that way," which, of course, is quite the opposite of business innovation.

If you always do what you've always done, you will always get what you've always had. Institutions need a linear control over a manageable business, whatever that business is. As a result, it's inevitable that companies first get stuck, and then get Excession Evented to oblivion, just like Blockbuster.

Another reason companies prefer answers over questions is because questions are scary, and sometimes painful! Everyone survived the past, but no one knows if they're going to survive the future. Therefore, if you can make your future look very much like your past, then you're much more likely to be in control a bit and to manage it. At least that is the thinking process.

People are very afraid of change. They like the idea of change, but the reality of it is often too frightening for them to deal with. In cases such as these, organizations may indeed change, but at a very slow rate, so it's not quite as frightening to them. A company's culture is only a collection of individuals, whose emotions influence their decisions. As a result, they will often only change at the slowest rate they can possibly get away with.

* * *

These tales of change bring us to Sisyphus. In Greek Mythology, Sisyphus was condemned by the Gods to push a rock to the top of the hill constantly. Once the rock got to the top of hill, it would roll the bottom, and he would have to walk down the bottom of the mountain and push it back up the mountain again. He was condemned for all eternity to do it again and again.

For many people, there is comfort in this repetition. They know what they need to do. It produces an entirely repeatable action, whether it's pointless or not, and it makes the days go by. They know that the rock will get to the top of the mountain, and it will roll down, quarter after quarter, year after year.

There is a joke in sales that goes, doing a quarter of any NASDAQ company is a bit like running a 400-meter race. You start the race and you run around the track. As you come down to the final stretch, you have to start running faster because the clock is running down. As you pass the start/finish line, you're absolutely exhausted. The gun then goes off for the beginning of the next race, except the next race has to be slightly faster than the last one. If you didn't hear the gun go off, it was you they shot. If you want evidence, simply go to LinkedIn and look at salespeople's tenure.

We call it the death march, and pretty much any salesperson will identify with it. The numbers just get harder and harder until at some point you either wear out, or break, or the company has had enough of you and you part ways. You then join a different company, reset the clock, and away you go again.

Now, this is dispiriting perhaps, but a long period of time will pass between the point where you stop that race and the one where you can't run any faster. New things come along, new products and new initiatives that will help you get that extra 10% that they want.

As a result, you could live the life that you actually want to live with family and friends and vacations. You could be relatively safe in the knowledge that if you do these numbers of actions, you will come up with a good result that will continue to have you employed.

This attitude can be scaled up from an individual to an entire organization and it still works. The sales number for every company is simply a multiplier of the number of sales people you've got by running the system described. Having lots of different sales people enables you to predict the number more accurately because the peaks and troughs for each individual will be less. This ultimately has to do with the fact that most human beings are more comfortable being train drivers than train designers.

You could say to most people, "Here is a blank sheet of paper. Design a train." They wouldn't have a clue where to start. I think it would be a little Pavlov dog-like in the sense that it would all be consuming. They wouldn't know how to interact with it, what to do to get to the result. In comparison, driving the train is relatively simple. You shovel the coal in it, you turn up a few knobs and away the thing goes. There's comfort in that.

Intellectually, most people are more interested in driving the train. Most people do not want to spend their lives thinking about their work. They want to get off at work at 6 p.m. They want to go home and have dinner with their family, and they want to watch *The Apprentice* or *America's Got Talent*.

* * *

A contrarian, of course, would handle a Sisyphus situation much differently. Instead of pushing the rock to the mountaintop *ad infinitum*, the contrarian would likely say, "Why am I pushing this? What's the purpose? Maybe this rock shouldn't be pushed at all." It's extremely liberating to think this way.

You see, one of the major problems with pushing the rock is that all you get to see is the front of a rock. This is one of the reasons companies get blindsided. They don't give themselves enough time to think. The vast majority of people, individually and within companies, generally equate "busyness" with success.

Every salesperson I've ever met has had a slow period in terms of sales. They don't go, "Is this the right system?" They go, "I'm going to pedal harder. I'm going to grind out a result." This is not some zero-sum game. We are not boxing. There are not rules which you need to work by.

In boxing, if you're going to beat the other guy, you need to keep thumping harder than he's thumping you and just keep doing it until he goes down. But business does not work that way. If you run a boxing match like you run a business, you could leave the ring, go out to the parking lot, get in your car, drive into the stadium and run over your opponent. You're going to win the boxing match that way. Mike Tyson is probably not going to survive me driving over him in my Denali.

But if you play the game by the rules that other people have set, then you're probably going to lose at some point.

There is a strong argument that says, "Being busy is one of the worst things that any individual business can do." Because it stops you from *thinking*. I think that a lot of business people actually like that.

How many people do we all meet in our lives who can't wait to tell you how busy they are? "Our work's crazy. I've got all these projects." Well, are you being good to *any* of them? Have you ever considered that probably half of those projects shouldn't even be done? Well, of course, the answer is no. They haven't solved any of those things through because activity is the ultimate Sisyphus situation, where they would rather be busy than be thinking. I believe most people are rather afraid of thinking, which is surreal to me. They want to do the same thing over and over again, like Sisyphus.

As for me, the last thing I *ever* want to do is anything twice. I want to spend my entire life doing everything once. Once I do a thing, I then automate it to the point where it could be done without me. The thing I'm really good at in business is *thinking*, but the thing I'm really bad at is *doing*. I get bored really quickly, but most people do not.

In the science fiction story *The Hitchhiker's Guide to the Galaxy* by Douglas Adams, there is an alien species called Belcerebrons who are such brilliant thinkers that the rest of the galaxy despises them for it. As a result, the Belcerebrons have telepathy forced upon them by the rest of the galaxy.

Now, every single thought the Belcerebrons have is broadcast to everyone within a 200-yard radius, whether they want to or not. The only way to stop that is to speak loudly and continuously about the weather, what was on television, what they saw on Facebook, what their favorite band was, etc. That was the only way they could stop thinking.

Most of our culture is about spending as little time thinking as possible because people are frightened of it. And like the Belcerebrons, we tend to fill our world with trivial distractions to avoid the fear of thought.

※　※　※

So, what does it take to be Netflix? First, stop with "magical thinking." If posed with hard questions, "We've always done it this way" is not an acceptable answer. Working harder isn't the right answer either. Instead, try giving yourself time to think about your business. Think about what business you're really in. These are critical points that deserve your attention. But in order to get there, you'll have to stop clinging to your old beliefs. That may be the hardest step of all.

What if your business model is being changed by some outside organization, for example, Blockbuster by Netflix? The idea that your business will continue to roll along is highly unlikely. You can't sit there and say, "We'll milk it to some period of time." This is going to prevent you from seeing a solution.

You don't need a crystal ball in cases like these. But remember, "In the land of a blind, the one-eyed man is king." You don't need to be all-knowing, you just need to be one step ahead of your competition. The best way of doing that is to look at the world around you, maintain awareness of other markets, and try to identify which markets may be coming in to yours.

If you need inspiration, look no further than the scientific community. For the past few years, they have been blending together people from different disciplines to gain greater overall perspective. I think that this is something that businesses need to think about.

One company I used to work for was in the video conferencing industry. Everyone we looked to hire, guess what? They ran a video conferencing business, too. So we hired people who already knew all the same stuff we did. We ended up with a company where everyone already thought the same way.

Here's how it worked. We'd call candidates in for interviews, then we would ask them some questions. They would know the answers, and they would come up with the same answers we did. Well, that sounded like just the right kind of people we would like to hire. We would also, and businesses do this all the time, hire people who look like ourselves. This is the wrong way to go about business.

It is far preferable to have people who are different; who have come out of different disciplines, different worlds of business, and are also culturally different from you.

No one in middle-class Austin, Texas, is thinking about how to solve problems in the third world. We don't even know that these problems exist. But if we hire some folks who came out of Africa or out of India, for example, then they'd be asking different questions. We'd much more likely come up with an interesting answer if different questions were being asked.

Steve Jobs said, "We don't hire clever people and tell them what to do. We hire clever people and have them tell *us* what to do"

We have talked a bit about 10× increases. Now let's look into how to achieve it.

If I had a 100-pound weight and I asked you have to lift it above your head, chances are you're probably going to be able do it. If I then said to you, "Next time the weight is going to go up by 10%. It will be 110 pounds." If you had struggled with 100 pounds, well, 110 pounds *might* be doable.

If I increased the weight by another 10%? It may be getting harder to do, but you're not going to think differently about the problem. You might go and do some weight training. If I told you that we're going to go from 100 pounds to 150 pounds over the next six months, you'd probably go out to the gym, you'd work out, and you'd get better at it. Chances are, you're going to lift it.

But what if, after you lifted the 100-pound weight above your head and put it down, I said, "By the way, the next time we do this, you need to lift 1,000 pounds above your head." You would think about the problem entirely differently. You would never sit there and say, "Right. I'm going to go to the gym and start working out." It would be pointless! No one can lift 1,000 pounds above their head. So the methodology you would use would have to be fundamentally different. You would listen to the question more closely.

Instead of weight training, you might work on getting yourself some sort of exoskeleton, or a forklift of some kind. You might try designing a new process. Whatever you did, you wouldn't be trying to hit the gym to make yourself a bit stronger, because all the training in the world wouldn't help you lift 1,000 pounds.

To achieve this leap from 10% growth to 10× growth, businesses need to move away from the idea of linear growth. They need to stop thinking that they can do the same things they've done before. Typically, businesses will think that doing the same thing, just more efficiently, is good enough. But instead, they need to fundamentally decide that they are in a different business altogether and need to work their problem out in an entirely new way.

To *really* work things out in a new way and advance to 10× growth, the first thing you should do is ask yourself: "Do I even need to lift this 1,000 pounds?"

✳   ✳   ✳

Robert Solow is a Nobel Prize winning economist who, even today in his 90s, is working at MIT. For a long time, Solow has held the position that productivity continues to increase at a fairly linear way.

Solow also noted that, since the Industrial Revolution, there have been three waves of technological change that really increased the rate of productivity change: Transportation, electrification, and telecommunications. But Solow also stated that the funny thing about technology is that it seems to exist everywhere except within the productivity figures. There's not a big step change in the way that electrification

changed the economy. The Internet and computerization have not changed the economy that much, either.

Instead, the economy continues to grow in a relatively linear manner. Solow's question is, "Why is that?"

There are a number of possible answers. Perhaps it's too early; maybe we haven't had the opportunity yet for these numbers to be set. Having said that, we have had the Internet, in one form or another, for about 25 years. You'd expect to see the numbers by now. So I find that hard to believe.

The next possibility is that maybe the Internet is simply not that big a deal; maybe it's not that important compared with the other technological changes. Personally, I struggle to accept that harnessing a few billion more minds into the universal collectiveness does not have a fundamental change in the way that the world works. So I reject that possibility as well.

The third answer that I think would be reasonable to look at would be, we're simply not using it well enough. I would argue that that is the problem of our time.

What we have done with our business models to date, with a few exceptions, is to take an old business model, slap it on the Internet, and expect it to produce fundamentally different results...which of course it didn't. It's not surprising that we've done it this way. Almost every time we come up with a new technology, it looks like the old model. The first cars were called "horseless carriages" because that's what they looked like. Eventually, they evolved into something different.

Today's early self-driving cars are the same: They look like regular cars. But really, if you have an entirely autonomous self-driving car, why would you want that? I'd much prefer it to look like a living room on wheels.

As a result, I would argue that Solow is right. The Internet does *not* bring a step change in productivity growth, and the reason why is because we're not using it correctly.

There are exceptions that are beginning to show what can

be achieved with the Internet. Amazon and Netflix are at the top of the list. They are utilizing the Internet in a more efficient way than any of their competitors. Everybody else is taking their horse-and-cart and putting it on the freeway... where it still does five miles an hour. They have a wide open freeway before them, but they fail to redesign the idea of what is possible. Meanwhile, Amazon and Netflix have realized that they can completely change the paradigm of their core business, and are winning as a result.

An organization like Amazon was an Internet-based organization without brick-and-mortar stores that sold print books. They realized if they could work out a way to deliver the book using the Internet as a medium, then they would have a massive advantage over their competitors. As a result, e-books are highly profitable for Amazon, and a total catastrophe for Barnes and Noble.

Barnes and Noble cannot come up with an e-book because as soon as they do, it fundamentally breaks their business model. It makes no sense for a company with brick and mortar stores to sell you a book or a device that means you never need to go to the store again. But they did it anyway because they had to. Their investors told them, "You have got to look like Amazon." Even though it makes no sense! If they're successful with NOOK, then they will put their own bookstores out of business. If they're not successful with NOOK, then Amazon will put their bookstores out of business. Either way, Barnes and Noble bookstores are out of business. Which is a shame because I'm a huge Amazon fan, but I love bookshelves, too.

A possible solution for Barnes and Noble is to change the rules. Make their book stores more like libraries or local book stores. Make the store the center of the book community. Many people love simply being around books. If Barnes and Noble can crack that, then they could have a business model. Simply chasing Amazon looks like an unlikely route to success.

* * *

Like Barnes and Noble, Kodak is another organization that failed to realize what a paradigm shift of their core business could achieve. Now, it's not that Kodak were fools. Kodak invented the world's first digital camera sensor as far back as 1976. Despite this, the technologies needed for the sensor to be useful simply didn't exist at the time.

Let's break this down. If I'm going to have a digital camera, ignoring whether it's in a phone or any other device, what is needed for it to be a useful piece of technology? It needs to have a display on which to show a photograph. It needs both high quality screens on people's computers and high quality screen on the cameras themselves.

Next is needed high-performance processing. This applies to both the camera itself and the computer. Only with good processing power will it be able to take and manipulate the pictures effectively. Large amounts of low-cost storage are needed for all these files. Good quality, high-compression file formats will need to be available widely, so standards will need to be ratified and adopted. These will allow pictures to be taken and compressed in a format or into a form that's small enough to be useful and convenient.

Color printers will be required to be able to print these pictures. Otherwise, all they do is sit on my camera or sit on my computer forever. For it to really take off, Internet access speeds need to be good enough that images can be shared with friends and family. This is the real killer application for digital photography: The ability to share it with others.

Kodak could make a digital sensor, but they weren't in the hard drive business or the display business or the Internet business or the computer business or the color printer business. As a result, they could have one piece of the puzzle, but not all the others.

What ultimately crushed Kodak was that all the technologies we just mentioned did eventually become possible, but Kodak failed to see their significance. They believed that the market that was about to be produced, digital cameras, was going to be one twentieth the size of the market they were presently in. So they couldn't even fit their business into this new market.

So what Kodak did was two things: Firstly, they sold off Eastman Kodak, the chemicals division of Kodak, as a separate entity. Secondly, they dismantled the company as quickly and as reasonably as they could to fit into the new market dynamic.

The argument that Kodak was a failure because they missed the digital photography Excession Event is unreasonable. That isn't a fair assessment at all. They did a great job in a position of extreme problems. They went bankrupt in an extremely organized way. In chapter 11, they sold off a lot of their patents and they spun off a Fortune 500 business. Otherwise, they folded up the tepee and slinked off the reservation in as controlled a manner as possible. Very rarely has that ever happened before. Almost every company that's found itself in a similar position has exploded. Kodak, instead, was more of a controlled implosion.

* * *

THE TENTH MAN

In the 1930s, the Jews in Europe heard rumors of Nazi death camps. These rumors were so horrendous that they thought it couldn't possibly be true. Despite their denial of this horrible reality, we all know what happened to them in the Holocaust. Then, in 1973 Yom Kippur War, the Syrians, Jordanians and Egyptians were all moving their heavy weapons around and all the generals said, "It's nothing. There's not going to be a problem at all." Nobody asked, "But what if that's wrong?" As a result, the Jews nearly lost the whole of Israel in 1973 in the Yom Kippur War.

The Israeli Defense force developed a concept they called "The 10th Man." The concept: If everyone in an organization agrees on a course of action, whatever that course of action is, it must always be one person's duty—whether they believe it or not—to argue the opposite. To be the contrarian who is prepared to sit there, be unpopular, and say to the organization, "You're wrong. This is an issue and we must fix it." Then it's their job to try and convince the rest of the organization.

If an organization has a militaristic mindset of making more and more decisions at a more and more senior level, whoever sticks his hand up at that point becomes the contrarian...and is likely to get himself shot. But if you have a "10th Man" culture within an organization, then questioning the status quo becomes routine. In theory, this would be a senior member of staff who probably doesn't have anything to lose by being the contrarian. In American business, Boards of Directors are *supposed* to play that 10th Man role, but they rarely do. It should be the role of Chairman. Increasingly, the role of Chairman and CEO are combined under the guise of stopping factions from forming. However, the counter to this is the culture of groupthink.

Companies who wish to prepare for Excession Events would be wise to nominate a 10th man whose job it is to turn around and say to the CEO, "No, your answer doesn't make sense and you must consider another one." Even if the CEO turns out to be right, the contrarian mustn't be penalized. Because it's not a personal issue; they're just doing their job and playing their role as the 10th man.

The 10th man is nothing new; the idea exists in many other forms, as well. On a Navy vessel, the Executive Officer who reports to the Captain is the "designated contrarian." He is responsible for telling the captain of all the possibilities and consequences of their actions. The First Officer enacts the Captain's orders; the Executive Officer gives the Captain options.

In British politics, the Prime Minister's Questions, or PMQs, occur every Wednesday. The Prime Minister will stand in the middle of the House of Commons, and the opposition gets to ask him or her questions. Those people are known as the "Loyal Opposition"—loyal to the Queen, who is the Head of State, and loyal to the country. No one is suggesting that they're anything other than patriots. But it is their job to pick holes in the government's arguments, and it works very effectively. It forces the Prime Minister to have thought through and justified a position to themselves that can be explained and justified to others.

Despite these many forms of 10th Man culture through history and around the world, it is lacking from business today. This problem needs to be corrected. If you don't have a 10th Man, then organizations fall into groupthink; into the law of least resistance: "We're all in this together." Or, as Ben Franklin observed, "We all hang together or we'll all hang separately." When the chips are down, especially with looming Excession Events, organizations will all hang together. They often feel that if they express a contrary viewpoint, they will be contributing to splitting the company apart—when, in reality, that contrary viewpoint may be their salvation.

"52% of the Fortune 500 firms since the turn of the millennium are gone."

Where we're at today is, businesses will often have a room full of people saying yes to each other. It started from day one when they were hired because they look like, sound like, and have similar opinions to the person who interviewed them.

This vulnerability can be fixed. You need to hire outside of your business world, your gender, your class and your country. But also, once you have a diverse team on board, you still need to build the right culture. I believe you have to enshrine into the culture of the company someone whose job it is to be the joker: The guy who points out that "the king's not wearing any clothes." They must be able to contradict freely, without fear that doing so will get them locked up in the tower.

This "Joker" within your organization will be a key contributor to your Excession Event management, serving as a sentry who guards against the unexpected by constantly questioning the status quo.

ELEVEN

Learn Continuously

"God made the idiot for practice, and then he made the school board."

— MARK TWAIN

A key strategy in identifying and managing Excession Events is to be constantly learning. This type of education doesn't have to take place in a school. By fostering a mindset of learning, we never get stuck in our worldviews.

Ben Franklin, a passionate learner, never went to university. He started working at the age of 12 in a print press. School was not a big part of his life, but he continuously learned. My favorite line about Benjamin Franklin is old, but it's still amusing to me. He was once getting chewed up by his local priest because he fell asleep in church. The vicar said to him, "Mr. Franklin, if you can't stay awake during my sermons,

I'd rather you didn't come at all." Ben Franklin said, "Okay. That's great." He never went to church again.

Clearly, Franklin was a contrarian who defied the status quo. This attitude served him well: By questioning everything, he discovered the Gulf Stream, invented the lightning rod, and created bifocals, among hundreds of other significant achievements.

Franklin lived in an era where a man could be a polymath, a Renaissance man, a "Scientist of Everything." This was easier back then because all you needed was enough time and enough access books to read and learn. Because we knew so little in Franklin's era that it was possible for all of that information to fit in one person's head. A well-stocked library of the time might contain a few hundred books. Thomas Jefferson's extraordinary library was sold to Congress in 1815 and contained 6,000 books.

Today, that isn't true anymore. If you talk to a doctor and then you talk to a specialist, the answer you get from the specialist can be completely different. The General Practitioner doctor probably learned a piece of medicine 15 years ago that had a half-life that may not hold up today. What they know may no longer be relevant. So the whole idea of having any education in which you *learn* things and then a working environment in which you *do* things means that all your information will ossify. So-called "knowledge" will become part of the groupthink, and will stay there, regardless of whether or not it is true.

This is why we must consciously try to be wide ranging learners. Our education system is not on board with this. You don't get a degree. You get a degree in marketing, or a degree in computer science, or a degree in astronomy, or a degree in whatever. You don't get an *overall* degree because it would, in some sense, be viewed as meaningless. But actually, having an *overall* degree that gave you the ability to see the connections between different things would be great.

Progress today in science, and therefore in technology, comes from an expiration effect. James Burke once observed that the information in the deserts *between* the disciplines is where there is such fertile ground now. A computer scientist may know a bunch of things and the next discipline along also knows a bunch of things. Where it gets interesting today is that there's data that each one doesn't know that the other one would find useful.

The Dead Sea Scrolls have been unintelligible since being rediscovered in 1947 because they are fragile and many of them are burnt. Archaeologists didn't know what to do with them. They tried unwrapping a few, but they were just too fragile. Then a man who built MRI scanners found out about the project and said to the archaeologists, "I know how to do this. I could read your scrolls even though they're wound up, even though they're burnt." So now they're using MRI scanners to scan and read 4,000-year-old documents.

It worked because two worlds that would never normally have met interacted with each other. There are a lot of opportunities for groups with different disciplines to work together. Exobiology as a discipline exists, which is a little surprising considering that there isn't any known exobiology.

Bringing astronomers, geologists and biologists together to work means we can learn an awful lot more about the universe than we could when each one was looking at it on their own. You show an astronomer a series of Martian rocks, he doesn't know what he's looking at. But bring in a geologist and a biologist, and suddenly you've got, "This looks like coral beds, and therefore this location may have had coral in it before." Knowledge, shared across disciplines, opens amazing opportunities.

Learning doesn't end the day you graduate. The world is always at our fingertips. Many people go and join a gym and do an hour's worth of exercise, but they don't go and do an hour's worth of mental exercise. I'm not talking about Sudoku, either. Go read a book about something that's actually happened, learn about a thing that isn't in your house, or go and watch "the other guy's news."

When I left school at 18, my headmaster said, "Dudley, you'll never amount to anything." It was a lovely thing for a headmaster to say. Three years later, while selling fax machines, I got my equivalent of my W2 form. It was a large sum of money. So I faxed my old headmaster my "W2," circled my salary for the year, and wrote on it, "From the boy who would never amount to anything." As a 21-year-old fax machine salesman, I out-earned the high school headmaster.

The whole education system and I had not seen eye to eye at all. Despite this, since dropping out of school, I have been on a path of continuous learning. This is something I think I learned from my father. After he left the RAF, he went to night school for 10 years to try and get some of his qualifications and screwed it all up. He was no good at passing the exams.

And yet, my father went on to be an unqualified success, and he always instilled in me the idea that learning things can be fun. There's an excitement about the world. From the time I was a child, I never bought into theological beliefs. I have just always been interested to know how the universe works. As a result, I've just been trying to figure it all out ever since.

As a child on a quest for understanding, I used to take things apart, but I could never put them back together again. That was my father's job. More importantly, I started reading as widely as possible. I wasn't interested in any one topic; I never became a specialist, and I was never funneled down one path of knowledge.

The fact that I never believed in school learning has only helped me in life. In a world where changes are happening so fast, and all the knowledge in the world is at our fingertips, it's crucial that we don't memorize facts and get stuck in our ways. And yet, that is what our education system teaches us.

It seems most people believe school is where you learn, and work is where you do things.

Personally, I seem to have forgotten to stop learning. As this book hopes to show, that's the only winning strategy in the modern era.

How do we start to learn continuously? Some people stand on stage and say, "You should innovate." But that is useless because it is not actionable. It's not telling you what to do. So I want to give you some advice on what to actually do, and it starts with consuming information as widely as possible. Try to know less and less about more and more.

When you consume as widely as possible, it means that the nature of the Excession Event becomes less important. It could be originating in science, in technology, or in society. If you are versed across all of these areas, you can recognize the event sooner and manage it more effectively. Critically, and this is the bit that really matters: You can see the *connection* between the Event and the next piece of technology.

The ability to see connections in many puzzle pieces matters more than being an expert in the individual piece. Therefore, the wider you read, the more likely you are to cover more connections; to see *more* of the pieces of the puzzle that may come together to produce the next big leap forward.

If I had seen "good quality screens" and "digital sensor technology," but I haven't seen "cellular phones," then I would have only thought that the world would have lots of digital cameras in it. I wouldn't have understood that they could have been connected into phones. As a result, I would have been into trouble. Or if I had seen "cellular technology" and "battery life," but not "screen technology," then I would only see a world full of cell phones that look like Nokias from 1999: A wonderful battery life and we would talk forever, but I wouldn't be able to play a game on it or look at photographs or any of those things. So I would have come up with *some* of the story, but not *all* of it...and therefore I would have missed the whole point in it.

The wider your scope of knowledge, the more equipped you are to detect these connections. Also, as your scope of knowledge widens, as you look more and more outside of your own world, you're less likely to get blindsided by Excession Events, because you're already aware of many different subjects.

* * *

Next, you must read outside your existing positions and interests. Read about things that you are not familiar with. Many people will not read an article or a piece or a book about a topic they don't already know something about.

My father was a serious engineer. When you spoke to someone like my father, he would keep explaining it until you either did understand it or faked that you understood it. What I would do as a child, and I think what most people would do, was to simply nod. My father would just get frustrated and stop with most people, but with me, I had to fake that I understood what he was talking about until the point where I *did* understand what he was talking about.

My father would keep going on a topic and I would keep listening. Then, because he would explain in three or four or five or 12 or 150 different ways, eventually the message got through and I began to connect the dots. At age five or six, I vividly remember my father explaining to me how electricity worked. He would just explain until I said I understood. He wouldn't shout, he wouldn't raise his voice, he would just keep doing it until you just agreed that you understood. Then if you were really unlucky, he would then say, "You understand? Explain it back to me."

"Don't let schooling interfere with your education."
— MARK TWAIN

This ability to listen, to nod, and to learn by osmosis is a talent that most people do not have. I think what a lot of people will simply say is, "I don't know anything about that," at which point, they shut off the idea of learning anything new.

The idea of being ignorant and being okay with that is something my father always hated. I would never let him see that in me, so I wouldn't do it. I think that put me in a great place for the modern world, where ignorance is entirely optional.

If you have access to the Internet, you can know any topic. You don't have to be a world-class. I'm not expecting you to be an Alan Turing level cryptographer, but you can at least know enough about a topic that you could discuss it with people for five minutes. That allows you to see the connection between that topic and another one. I think that's what matters. The gaps between the topics are where the really interesting stuff happens. It also means an expert is likely to be prepared to spend more time with you if you have something to contribute.

* * *

So how, in our busy lives, can we find the time to be continuous learners?

A subscription can be a great way to start, and if I could recommend one publication to read above all else, it would be *The Economist*. *The Economist* is available both as print and digitally, including a podcast. So if you commute to work, you can get through an issue in a week, which is perfect because then the next one comes along.

I knew nothing about economics when I subscribed to *The Economist* 15 years ago. I was reading all sorts of things in their columns about currency fluctuations and about subprime mortgages. I couldn't grasp it, but I kept listening. Then after a while I realized I *did* understand every word of it. The general educational system does not work that way.

The world of Podcasting is extraordinarily broad. Each Podcast can appeal to only a small specialist group and still be successful. Even ExcessionEvents.com has a Podcast. The barrier to entry is so low that anyone can get involved.

The general education environment demands that you understand every step. Meanwhile, if you're an adult learner it may be better to dive into all that information and let it soak in through osmosis. You don't have to learn it all. But you can learn a lot by simply being in the room with all the right people. That's effectively what *The Economist* is.

The Economist is not just about money. It's about business and about politics, and therefore it's about the ideas that run our world today. *The Economist* does a fantastic job of talking to you like you're an intelligent, well-read, reasonable human being, but without you having to be an expert in any of it. For example, they have a science section where, if it were a science journal, you would already have to have a degree in the topic to understand it.

If a topic in *The Economist* was in the *Wall Street Journal*, then it will only be about finances. If it was in the *New York Times*, it would be written for an eighth-grader. *The Economist* never assumes that you're an expert in all the topics, and it does a truly brilliant job of finding that middle ground of intellectual rigor without having to be a scientific expert in whatever the topic is.

The BBC radio for podcast called *In Our Time* is another I would recommend. The podcast is weekly and hosted by Melvyn Bragg. It covers the most diverse set of topics you can imagine. In the span of a few weeks, *In Our Time* might cover

Zen Buddhism, Aesop, the Hessian Revolution, Thomas Paine, Wealth of Nations, Dark Matter, Julius Caesar, the Philosophy of Solitude...it is worth listening to to broaden one's thinking.

Melvyn invites three experts in on the topic, and then he learns from them. Bragg is not the expert, but what he's great at doing is asking these people the questions that matter. Then they go and answer the questions for him. If they get a bit longwinded or boring or off topic, Bragg pulls them back. He understands the information that *matters*. He understands narrative, he understands the questions to ask, and then he lets the experts—who could never perform his role—be the ones who come up with the absolute right answer. He plays the simple man, the contrarian.

HBR, *Harvard Business Review*, is good because it's probably got the latest and best ideas about management structures and way that you actually enact any of them. It's probably useful to at least understand how other people are thinking.

You need to read widely enough that you could have a reasonable position on your ideas that is defendable. Not defendable just for today, but defendable until the facts change, at which point your opinion must change.

*   *   *

Get a mentor or become a mentor.

A mentor is a very important thing for people to do for no other reason than it gives you someone that you want to impress. If you let yourself down, it's *easier* if you surround yourself with people who don't know anything, or people who don't even notice. But if you have a mentor, and if they're doing their job right, they will question you. So, effectively, having a mentor is like having your very own personal 10th Man. They'll actually make you justify your thinking.

This role of the mentor seems especially important today, when most people's opinions come from somebody else. Media in the modern era is the perfect example; they've gone from reporting the news, to doing the analysis for you, to now simply telling you what to think. And people believe it, because it's easier when you don't have to learn anything for yourself. You can simply wait until whomever you've chosen to be your surrogate thinking machine turns up and tells you what's what.

I would encourage people beyond all else to move away from that. A good mentor can help because this is someone who, when you express a position, will ask you, "Why? Why do you think that?" I think that that is an extraordinarily powerful idea because it makes you actually justify your thinking to both others and to yourself.

There are so many people who have these ideas that may be false. But because no one had ever questioned them on their idea, it could sit there like a bubble in the room. I think a mentor's job is to go along and prick that bubble; to see if it pops. If it doesn't pop, it might be a relatively valid idea, or at least a defensible position.

When you *are* a mentor, you get to be the 10th Man, and work on your questioning skills. This is a good thing in itself. Most of the time, when you're questioning somebody else's assumptions, you also, by nature, end up questioning your own. You get into this mode of questioning that can have so many benefits in both personal and business affairs.

Being a mentor or having a mentor are effectively the same thing. I've mentored people in the past and I've learned things from them because they lived differently; they may have grown up in a different culture or a different time. This is incredibly valuable because you get to see how the world works from somebody else's perspective.

* * *

As you're reading this, you are almost certainly saying "I'm too busy to be a mentor." Or, "I'm too busy to read." But trust me, it's important to make time for these activities, especially if you want to successfully manage Excession Events.

Now, for those of you who allegedly have no time: Did you know the average American spends 159 hours a month in front of the television? And further, did you know that the human mind is as active watching television as it is when asleep? Television is the opiate of the masses!

Stop with the television. Nothing good is coming from watching television. Your shows are doing nothing but robbing you of time. If you want to free up an awful lot of time, simply stop watching television.

The second way to leverage your time is to take advantage of your empty time in the car. Most people commute, and they listen to "JB and Sandy In the Morning," which is normally ludicrous jokes about famous personalities and traffic reports. What a waste! You can do much better than your local radio show. Our morning and evening commutes present the perfect opportunity to listen to podcasts of important things, like *The Economist* or *Harvard Business Review*, or any other number of great publications on a regular and reasonable basis.

Finally, it is helpful to put time in your diary or in your calendar for mental exercise. People will say, "On Tuesdays at 7, I go to the gym for an hour." But very few people do this for their minds. Why not?

Really, excuses like, "I can't afford it and I don't have the time," just don't work. They're not reasonable statements. People have tons of time. They just choose to use it in a series of meaningless ways, not the least of which is following celebrity culture, which is basically living vicariously through a bunch of morons. Our modern era is filled with meaningless distractions such as these, which makes it harder to focus on what's really important. But the act of learning has been made so easy by our modern era as well. All you need is a book, or some earphones in your iPod, and you can learn something. Make it a priority.

* * *

"Life's most persistent and urgent question is, 'What are you doing for others?'"
— MARTIN LUTHER KING, JR

The best option for continuous learning is to always be *doing* things, not merely consuming things. Consuming is absolutely passive. You can just sit there and the next TV show will come on, whether you're alive, dead, or in a food coma. There is no learning going on during consuming. This includes the mindless consumption of ideas.

If you only consume ideas and you don't *do* anything, then you're not actually getting outside of your own head. You're not examining your position. You're not being forced to defend your position in a robust way. This means you end up with a very delicate little bubble of ideas that you've consumed. You may become very nervous of ever getting out and showing these ideas to people, because you're worried that they would prick your idea bubble with a pin. It would be easy for them to do. People in this "idea bubble" mindset ultimately become very defensive of their positions.

While you're *doing* ideas, however, you learn. Because what learning allows you to do is *fail*. Because you're actively doing things, you have the opportunity to have your idea tested; in some cases, your ideas can be tested to destruction. You can't do if you just live in your own head. That's why *doing* matters.

The business community can be divisive in this regard. You start in a position with a bunch of other twenty-somethings, and as you age with them, you get richer with them. You start thinking at age 45 that everyone lives this way. You forget that there are folks who started their twenties on a different path, and have a very different outlook on life and have a very different set of life experiences.

I learned a lot from young people while volunteering. Even though I was able to help them in numerous ways, they helped me understand what it's like to be on $25,000 a year living in San Diego, which is an experience I've never had. Meeting people through these volunteer efforts certainly opened my mind to new ways of thinking.

Contributing to others beyond yourself is very good for your mental health. It gives you self-worth, it gives you somebody else to worry about, and it stops you doing the standard depressive stare at your own navel. It may give you a fresh perspective as well. All of this helps you to stay aware and to always be learning, which in turn may help you see the next big Excession Events before they happen.

TWELVE

The Future of "Free"

Traditionally, we lived in a world where rarity was valued. A perfect example of that would be in military technology, particularly since the industrialization of military technology in the 20th century. The more useful and powerful this technology became, the more likely it was to cost lots and lots of money. That gave many advantages to the people who could afford it and lots of downsides for those people who couldn't.

Consider the relative costs of the last 50 years' worth of strike fighters that the U.S. military has owned.

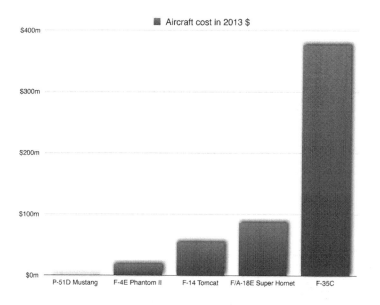

The cost of these fighter aircraft has risen exponentially over time. There is a quote by a U.S. Air Force general who states that, the way things are going, by the year 2050 the U.S. Air Force will be able to afford one aircraft.

At the time of this writing, a Joint Strike Fighter (F-35) program was proposed that would cost the U.S. government $1.5 *trillion over its lifetime in service.* It's just becoming inconceivable that that is a reasonable amount of money to spend for anything, where the chances are, you'll never actually use it.

The usual advantage for a wealthy country like the United States is its ability to maintain a technological advantage over its competitors. In this case, "competition" could be Russia, China, Al-Qaeda, ISIS, etc. Typically, the organization with the most resources wins because they could throw the most money at the problem. As what success looks like changes, then this model is disrupted.

The military industrial economy is changing as the distribution of technology is becoming inexpensive. Traditionally this wasn't the case. With the cost of research and development (R&D) coupled with finding that market, selling to it and advertising, you couldn't afford to do it.

In the case of military fighter aircraft, drones are now beginning to take over. Typically, drones are at least one and often two orders of magnitude cheaper than existing weapons platforms. By the time the Joint Strike Fighter is actually in service in quantity, its entire job will be replaced by drones.

Drones have all sorts of major advantages. No pilot means no rescuing the pilot if they get in trouble. They simply walk out of a Port-a-Cabin after a mission.

Drones are cheaper to buy and operate.

They will be better fighting machines than the manned aircraft. They don't have the wetware on board. Instead of having an on-board pilot, you have a pilot who can sit remotely in the Arizona desert and capably fly the drone. If he needs to get in a dogfight and pull 20 G turns he can do that—because the airframe can cope with it, even if a human pilot cannot.

Politically, boys coming home in body bags is unacceptable. Drones of all types change the geopolitical landscape. Since the Obama presidency, suspects are no longer taken to Guantanamo Bay. Not because the U.S. military isn't hunting for these people, but because they are all being killed in the field by drones.

Despite drones' advantages, work on the Joint Strike Fighter keeps moving forward. But what will ultimately happen is, by the time they build all the infrastructure for this Joint Strike Fighter, it will be redundant.

The British Royal Navy is now building two aircraft carriers for this Joint Strike Fighter. The people involved are already saying, "It's really too late for aircraft carriers to be useful at this point." But the decision to make the aircraft carriers was made politically 10 to 15 years ago, and drones weren't on the scene at the time.

You can't stop a project like this. It produces its own momentum. All the jobs, all the political will, all the contracts have been signed, and they've all got nasty clauses about breaking them. No politician wants to stop it. By the time those aircraft carriers are in the water and actually being used, which will be 10 years from now, the drones will have overtaken them completely. The Royal Navy is already testing drone take off and landings from carriers, so it is likely the ships will be converted.

Drones are an Excession Event that will utterly change both the military and political thinking of war.

The aircraft carrier conundrum isn't The British Royal Navy's fault. You can't go without a military force. You can't have zero defense for 15 years while we're waiting for the new technology. That's when somebody comes and invades you. Not making a decision is not a viable answer.

There are a lot of jobs and political will involved. There are a lot of bright people having made decent decisions at the time, which they are now emotionally and politically incapable of unmaking. If you had a brave political culture in both Britain and America, both countries would scrap the Joint Strike Fighter. But they won't, because they can't.

* * *

Drones' Excession of fighter aircraft is far from the only inexpensive technology that's changed the military. Another one happened 80 years ago with battleships. The British Royal Navy had a strategy at the turn of the 20th century that stated that they would build two battleships for each launched by a competitor navy. The Royal Navy effectively had a navy twice the size of the rest of the world combined.

It was ruinously expensive and hastened the demise of the British Empire.

If Russia, France, Germany, Japan or the United States built a battleship, Britain would build two because, for the British Empire, the navy was vitally important. You couldn't run an empire across the seas if someone could cut your country off from it.

Britain could not feed itself. It hasn't been able to for at least 200 years. As a result, if the shipping lanes were not kept open, Britain would starve to death. Germany nearly succeeded in doing just that with U-boats in the Second World War. Winston Churchill said the only thing that truly frightened him in the Second World War was the U-boats. He knew that they could starve Britain to death.

Battleships became ever larger. Partly to mount larger guns with longer ranges and partly to enable them to carry heavier armor to protect themselves against the enemies' guns. Each successive vessel became bigger, ever more expensive and ultimately too valuable to risk using. Even the loss of a few of these leviathans could cost a nation the war.

The greatest of these battleships were built by the Japanese. The Yamato, an example of the class, was half as big as the Bismarck, at over 72,000 tons, was equipped with nine 18-inch guns that could fire a one-ton shell over 26 miles. She was equipped with 162 antiaircraft guns and was ultimately sunk by torpedo bombers and dive bombers from

American aircraft carriers, which never got anywhere near being in range of the battleship's guns.

These battleships became ever more expensive, ever bigger, until the Second World War when the Japanese and Americans proved that aircraft carriers were the Excession Event for battleships. The Germans proved in the Atlantic that low cost submarines could also have a devastating effect, particularly on merchant ships.

Aircraft carriers are now facing the looming Excession Event of drones. It seems even the biggest and most expensive military technologies are not immune to the destructive power of Excession Events.

What the military industrial complex has always done is produce enormously expensive technologies, which typically, for the military, go up and up and up in price, and then for the normal non-military users, come down in price in a relatively predictable way.

❊ ❊ ❊

Instead of one incredibly expensive fighter plane, the world is now trending towards many inexpensive drones. This model is mirrored in the economy as well. Instead of selling one thing for a billion dollars, you can now sell a billion things for a single dollar and produce the same effect. This fundamentally turns economics on its head.

The Internet enables us to do two things that have never been available in history before. It gives us the opportunity to find customers incredibly inexpensively and it allows us to distribute products incredibly inexpensively. Not just software, which plainly can be delivered for almost zero cost, but also services and even physical hard technologies, because you can make this system so enormously efficient that the cost of the distribution is tiny relative to the cost of designing it in the first place.

Typically, a market would be considered a few tens or hundreds or thousands of customers. You might think you need to recoup all the research and development costs across a few hundred or a few thousand or a few tens of thousands of people. Consider optimizing that cost across hundreds of millions or *billions* of people. The R&D cost is so low per customer that the cost for each individual customer is very low to still have a successful product.

This brings us to the China model: It is much easier to sell one product for a billion dollars than it is a billion products at one dollar.

If you have a $1 billion product, then you can do an enormous amount of research to find the right customer for it. You can spend time finding the exact customer that product is worth a billion dollars to. You can do a lot of work to make certain that you built a product that was directly for them; that met their needs. You could throw bribes around to sell it too, if required. None of these things are possible if I need to be efficient.

The billion-dollar product enables you to have a highly inefficient sales model.

If you had to build a $1 product that you are going to sell to a billion people, then you need to be able to find the billion people to sell to at a dollar each. Then, how do you let them know that it exists? You've only got a dollar per person to spend and that includes your manufacturing costs, your distribution and your profits. How do you then make a billion? Then, how do you distribute those and still make any profit on the deal? It's a much harder problem, but the Internet has enabled technology that, for the first time, can make it happen. It doesn't happen in a traditional sales model.

If you're building a Joint Strike Fighter, there are 20 people on the planet who need to be convinced to buy it. It is the DoD's Head of the Defense Procurement, a few five-star generals, some important members of the Senate military procurement group, and that's about it.

You need one very expensive but very good salesman who probably is already a senator or the Ex Head of the Joint Chiefs of Staff. You don't need a marketing campaign in the same way for Joint Strike Fighters.

What happens is that organizations with very expensive products have *sales-led* business models. Then once products start getting cheaper, you move from a sales-led organization to a marketing-led organization.

Marketing-led organizations are typically built around

knowing who the customer is, and having a telesales person or a website that sells to that individual. This model doesn't personalize the product in any way. It isn't about a personal relationship. It's not about a salesperson within your organization spending a lot of time with a potential client because there's not enough profit in the deal for that to be worth it.

Marketing-led organizations would include companies like Salesforce or Microsoft. They sell reasonably priced products in the hundreds to thousands of dollars range, but those organizations are not individually catering their products to a customer. They have a very formulaic way of selling. It's a real marketing machine that does the work. There are some salespeople in these organizations, but at the end of the day they are certainly marketing-led, not sales-led.

Then the third group is brand-led. If you're buying a Samsung or LG Television, they don't know your name, but they advertise to you on television and online. They know what your persona is, your demographic, but not you personally. When you go to Costco they will make certain that their brand is on the end of the setup so that you see the Samsung TV before you see the LG TV. This group is driven by brand.

All three of those models are entirely valid. Businesses have a problem, however, when they try and move from being sales-led to marketing-led, and from marketing-led to brand-led. As soon as they make these shifts, it fundamentally changes the structure of their business. Those are major fear, pain, and danger points. Most organizations try to do everything they can to not ever have to cross those chasms.

They spend their time developing new products that are more expensive that allow their existing model to work for a while. This is fine, but eventually competition pushes down their pricing to the point where they have to introduce a new product that's more expensive, which then allows them to go through the cycle again.

Most organizations live in eco-cycles within their world but never cross from one to the other. When they do, it becomes extraordinarily painful for them.

*　*　*

Some other examples for the sales-led, marketing-led and brand-led business models include:

Boeing is a sales-led organization. No one reads *The Economist* and decides, "Oh, I'm going to buy a 737." You have a sales rep who comes and visits you if you're the buyer for Southwest or United.

Coca-Cola would be a perfect example of a brand-led organization.

The Virgin Group has done an excellent job of making certain that they sell you anything, but you're never buying a Virgin product. That's because there's no such thing as a Virgin product. They're all different things under the hood but what you're buying is the *brand experience* of Virgin.

They keep value up without necessarily becoming a marketing-led organization.

It's not hard to identify sales-led, marketing-led, and brand-led organizations. Finding an organization that has switched between those three worlds is very difficult because it's so dangerous to attempt it.

One company that tried to switch between worlds was IBM, when they made their move from mainframes to PCs. It nearly destroyed them. Many other people did a much better job than they did in the PC business.

Computer Associates, CA, tried to move from a sales-led to a marketing-led organization. They attempted it with low-cost products in the late 1980s, but quickly retreated up the value chain and sold rare but expensive technologies—and still do to this day. But in the late '80s and early '90s they had a torrid time of it.

Digital Equipment Corporation (DEC) would be an example of an organization that started as sales-led and then died during the time in which the market therein moved to a marketing-led model. Moving from high cost, low volume Mini Computing to the mass-produced commodity world of PCs with low differentiation killed them. Ultimately, they were swallowed by Compaq, who was in turn swallowed by HP.

If you want to *cause* an Excession Event in your market, and you can figure out how to make your business cross the chasms between models, then you have a new way to destroy your competition. If they tried to cross the chasm and were not properly equipped, they would fall in and perish. This is exactly what salesforce.com did to Siebel Systems. By transforming the world of CRM from a sales-led, long sales cycle market to a departmental, marketing-led business, Salesforce redefined the market.

In 2001, analysts were confidently predicting Siebel Systems would have a valuation of $66bn in five years—double its value at that time. A combination of a recession and the meteoric growth of Salesforce destroyed this valuation. Siebel was finally put out of its own misery with its acquisition by Oracle in 2005 for less than $3bn.

Here's an example: Compaq destroyed IBM's PC business. IBM was trying to move from a world of selling things to a world of marketing things. What Compaq did was simply start in the marketing-led world, not in the sales-led world. They never even tried to be in the sales-led world because their products weren't that expensive. As a result, they could redefine what success looked like in the PC world. IBM had to cross that chasm to compete, and they failed.

Dell moved the world of PCs from a marketing-led to a brand-led business. This was the Excession Event that Compaq could not cope with. In May 2002, Hewlett Packard (HP), an organization more comfortable in brand world, swallowed up Compaq. Today both HP and Dell are struggling in a post-PC world.

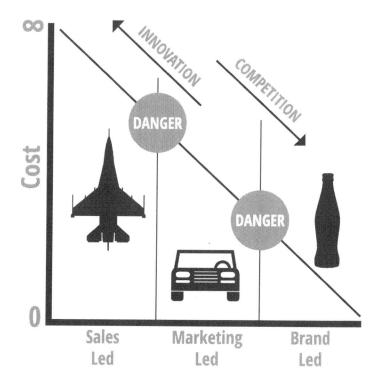

Technology just keeps getting cheaper. A television of today, in real terms, is less than 5% of a cost of a television from 1980. TVs of 1980 were around $1,000. That is $20,000 in 2015 money.

That's why everyone I know had the same TV for 20 years. They were a huge investment. Today, every bedroom has a TV. Televisions are now displaceable goods. We replace them every few years. They've become consumer items.

IKEA has turned furniture into fashion. Today, families buy

furniture as disposable fashion items: They keep it five or six years, throw it away and buy something new. But go back 80 years, before the Second World War, people hardly had any furniture. It's one of the reasons rooms were so small, because people couldn't afford to put anything in them.

Everything is becoming cheaper. This shift is not only fundamentally changing our economy, but also brewing massively destructive Excession Events on the horizon.

* * *

Thanks to the Internet, low manufacturing cost, and simple distribution, the cost of every consumer item in a modern American's life is trending towards zero...except for two items. These two items aren't getting cheaper. They are making us feel much less wealthy than we used to.

Healthcare and education.

The real cost of healthcare and education has dramatically lifted in the last 30 years. At the same time, the cost of everything else has fallen away.

Many factors have made healthcare expensive in the U.S. One factor: Doctors will do every test imaginable. This is partly because they don't want to be sued. But it's mainly because the American healthcare system is specifically designed around people wanting to give you every test and try every treatment because they get paid to do it.

The patient presently has no positive incentive to say, "No, no, no. All these tests are a waste of money. You shouldn't be doing it," because it's not *their* money. Meanwhile, the professional prescribing the healthcare is positively incentivized to make it as expensive as possible.

This paradox, coupled with the explosion in the number of healthcare products you can now buy, means that the cost of healthcare continues to skyrocket.

This may change because ObamaCare, for all of its faults, appears to finally be having some effect on the rampant cost of healthcare inflation. If written correctly, this legislation would have had a *massive* effect. But at least there is progress.

Education is getting more expensive as the universities are realizing that there's an awful lot of money being made by people with university degrees, and they want a piece of the action.

Universities understand that if you get a good degree from a top school, you will have enormous earning potential. They know that you need *their* piece of paper for that to be true. As a result, the universities are effectively taxing their students. They're saying, "You will get wealthy by taking our degree and we want some of it." That is becoming a major part of the problem.

The amount of facilities universities are building today is staggering. There's no actual positive incentive to save money because everyone has a university system that is designed around racing to the top.

Universities will not say to their students, "Our degree is not very good but that's okay. It's cheap." That's not much of a marketing ploy. However, in reality as *The Economist* has reported, where you get your degree makes very little difference on your overall life earnings relative to what subject you took. With that insight, you'd be much better off going to a cheap college and getting a computer science degree than you would going to an expensive college and getting a degree in art history.

The perception is that only the top 2% of graduates get the top 1% of jobs, although the evidence would suggest that is not true. For the first time, many people are waking up to the fact that they don't want multi-hundred thousand-dollar debts before they start work. This awakening could be an Excession Event for the Ivy League schools, who are looking at the scenario of, "More people want our degrees than we can actually give degrees to. As a result, we will keep upping the price until the market can't bear it anymore."

> *"The Internet is the first technology since the printing press which could lower the cost of a great education and, in doing so, make that cost-benefit analysis much easier for most students. It could allow American schools to service twice as many students as they do now, and in ways that are both effective and cost-effective."*
>
> — JOHN KATZMAN

* * *

With the two notable exceptions of healthcare and education, everything seems to be getting cheaper. Let's circle back to the business world and cover an important event that is changing the world of marketing: the advent of the "viral" concept. Besides being a game-changing Excession Event for business, virality is one of the most important forms of customer acquisition in the Internet age.

In a brand-led world, activities are thought of in a different way than a sales-led or a marketing-led world. In a brand-led world you need to be able to touch your customers without you touching your customers. You need your customers to *be* your sales organization because nothing else will be inexpensive enough for it to scale.

If I have to go and market to each one of my customers individually, it's too slow and it's too expensive. But if I can make my customers create a positive advantage by spreading my word for me, then I can take my product off like crazy. That helps with Metcalfe's Law.

The best way of producing a Metcalfe's Law effect is to produce a system that looks like the R-0 system used by virologists when looking at disease spread. The R-0 number defines how infectious something is. In the context of business, a product, a service, or a technology, how many times will it be "passed on" to somebody else? The higher that number, the more likely it is to be passed on to other people. This has become the single most important aspect of valuations of companies moving forward, particularly in the social communication space.

In the medical world, the common cold has an R-o number of 1.5. Each person who catches a cold is statistically likely to pass it to one and a half people. The Spanish Flu that swept Europe and Asia in 1919 immediately after the First World War had an R-o number of 3.5: Three and a half others on average caught the flu from each existing case. Spanish Flu killed over 50 million people, many more than the First World War. The Ebola virus has an R-o value of about 1.5 to 3, depending on the circumstances in which it's caught. Ebola is a highly contagious disease. The highest contagion of any disease in human history? Measles, which has an R-o value of between 12 and 18 depending on local conditions.

Measles is the primary reason that when the Europeans came to the Americas, they'd arrive in Native American villages to find everybody dead. The first infected European in an area would often be the last to see these people alive and could wipe out an entire population.

This same set of R-o rules from medicine can be applied to technology. Facebook is a perfect example. Look how quickly Facebook has swept throughout society. It's only 10 years old and over a billion people on the planet have a Facebook account. The reason it's useful is because Facebook didn't market. Our friends and family did it for them.

As a result, the valuations of the companies with high R-o numbers—like Twitter, Facebook, WhatsApp, Skype—are all enormously high.

If the R-o number dips below 1 then over time the system will die out. Think Myspace.

The problem with all of these models is they're predicated on the idea, just like we've discussed before, that these business will continue to grow in a linear way. Myspace had a huge valuation when Rupert Murdoch spent $540 million on it. He fell into the trap of linear thinking: He believed that since Myspace had grown in the past, it would always continue to grow. He fundamentally misunderstood what it actually was and, as a result, he ended up holding a pile of ashes.

The valuations of things like Twitter, Facebook, WhatsApp and Skype, for that matter, aren't predicated in any way on their present business models. They're predicated on some future that's linear. At some point someone will invent something that replaces Facebook. There are already warning signs that the number of people taking up Facebook, particularly among the young, is dropping. This should be viewed as ominous.

Instagram seems to be the next. My boys, ages 12 and 13, wouldn't touch Facebook with a barge pole. That's for old people. They're all Instagrammers. Maybe Instagram won't be the thing that kills Facebook but *something* will. It will go out of fashion and it will drop precipitously. It will be Excessioned out of existence by something else.

Facebook's present (June 2015) valuation is over $220bn. This valuation is not predicated on any material return on investment. It's predicated on some future valuation when every atom in the universe has a Facebook account and starts buying things from it. It doesn't seem very likely.

* * *

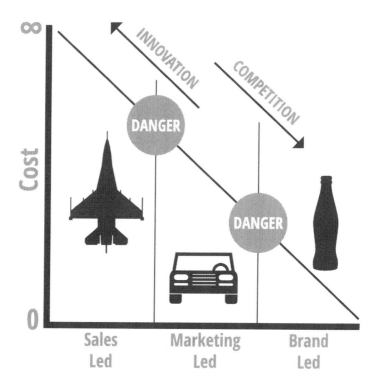

This new emphasis on exponential growth is fine and companies will self-correct. What's important is to avoid getting caught in danger zones where you're shifting along the axis but not using the right form of customer acquisition.

Businesses have to be careful. If you're in a position where your market is moving from sales-led to marketing-led, or from marketing-led to brand-led business, you have to understand that what you did previously cannot work in the new paradigm.

It's not an obvious change when your market shifts. You don't wake up one day and there's a storm out the window, "Right, we're now a marketing-led business, and we were a sales-led business before." What often really happens is you kind of fall into it when you weren't really looking.

You can change your proposition to get back up the value chain again, and sell to richer, more defined people. If you move from brand to marketing or marketing to sales, you know more and more about less and less people. You have a smaller market that's better defined by you. Then, if you move down the line, it's a bigger market that's less defined by you. It's also unknowable to you because the cost of acquisition is too high. This is the danger zone. You won't know it until you're in it. What you mustn't do is live in one world when you think and act as if you're in another.

Consider a business in the videoconferencing space. Five years ago, their market was dominated by the sale of $80,000 systems in meeting rooms. The average sales price for the manufacturer to their partners was $40,000. Today it's less than $10,000 on average, and dropping quickly. Having a sales rep that would go and see a customer and sell them a solution has now stopped being practical.

The sales-led model cannot work fast enough in that environment to make it reasonable. As an example, a sales rep would often have a target of $800,000 a quarter. If the average deal size was $20,000, forty of them hits quota. Forty deals. That's a lot of work, but it's probably doable. It's one every day and a half.

When the average sales price moves to $5,000, the number of deals required rises to 160 a quarter. The sales-led business model breaks. The number of opportunities you would have to have and the amount of meetings you would have to do would be so great it becomes impossible.

What people in this situation *shouldn't* do is think, "Right. Well, I have a business model. What I'm going to do is simply work harder." Working harder when your sales proposition has changed so dramatically is actually a losing strategy. You end up with a process where you start *working* harder instead of *thinking* more.

The less you think and the harder you work, the further down this rabbit hole you go.

If you're in this situation, you're not thinking, "I can't do this." It is, however, exactly what you should be acknowledging. What that videoconferencing market needed to do was take all the guys off the streets, stop everyone driving anywhere, and *use the technology itself* to sell the technology with a centrally-based sales organization that was much cheaper. Plus, since the centrally-based sales organization would actually use the videoconferencing communications technology to talk to the clients, they would be far more efficient. They needed to move from sales-led to marketing-led.

Instead of seeing one, maybe two clients a day, they could see 10 to 12 because they met them over video and did it from a cube. That's a fundamentally different way of working; a potential Excession Event in its own right. As it stands, salespeople are under the control of a marketing organization whose job it is to generate enough leads for those people to go and talk to.

Those who follow the status quo can't cope with this shifting world. That's one of the reasons why companies don't change. The head of sales is the most important man in the business. They are very unlikely to say, "You know what? This business model doesn't work anymore. I'll get my coat." He doesn't do that because he can't. Both emotionally and physically, he can't turn around and say, "This company does not need me anymore. I need to leave and you need to be successful without me." How many people are going to commit to that?

If the only tool you have is a hammer, everything is a nail.

Most people won't do that. These high-end sales guys and senior management of sales are workers, rarely thinkers. Thinking is just not what they do. They're doers. How many of them are going to put their hand up and say, "You don't need me anymore." They'll let the company make that decision. They're not going to volunteer it.

The companies don't make that decision because all the time the sales organization is coming up with a number, they don't care to know how they did it. Sales is often like a sausage factory. You know all these horrible things happen in sausage factories, but you don't want to know about them. That's true about sales organizations. The more you know about how sausages are made, the less likely you are to want to eat them.

*　*　*

A big Excession Event is happening right now, and it's turning sales-led organizations upside down. So how can an organization make changes that shift their model before they're Excessioned out of existence?

Depending on the market, a sales organization with big-hitter, expensive sales people driving fancy cars to convince clients may transition from a sales-led organization to a marketing-led organization. They might get there by switching to an in-house sales organization, like the videoconferencing company we discussed earlier.

In the marketing-led organization, we see a group of relatively inexpensive telesales people who can sell via video to all their customers instead of driving. They can see a lot more people at a lower cost per lead, with a marketing organization that feeds these video salespeople leads.

The next step, and it will happen to all these organizations, is to move from a marketing-led organization to a brand-led organization. Skype is the perfect example of that.

Skype's high R-0 rating enables Microsoft to build a business and customer base at low cost.

An extremely powerful aspect of the brand-led model: You can let customers have it for nothing, and then give them the option to you pay for extras if they want them. Probably 90% of the users pay nothing for it, but the company receives value out of them because those users go on to be their "sales organization."

To move from marketing-led to a brand-led sales model is just as disruptive, perhaps even more so. In brand-led, you have to be super-efficient in the way that you do business. If you're not, you end up like the *I Love Lucy* episode where Lucy and Ethel work the conveyor belt in the factory packing chocolates.

If you screw up your system under a brand-led model, it's just you and Ethel frantically sticking the chocolates in your dresses, in your pockets, under your hats, eating them…it all goes crazy. You can't afford to do that with a brand-led organization. It needs to be highly efficient and most organizations aren't highly efficient.

Imagine a sales-led organization that only makes one cake a year. That would be highly inefficient. It's okay because you got all this money you can play with. But once you've got all the way down to brand-led and you're only making $.01 per customer, you've got to be highly efficient. And if you've got Lucy running it, then the wheels come off, the factory closes, and no boxes come out of the back. Be wary of efficiency if you ever try to make the risky leap to a brand-led business. It's extremely hard.

THIRTEEN

The Future of Work

There is one looming event that is particularly powerful: Artificial intelligence. AI could be the ultimate Excession Event.

There's already a lot of talk among a number of scientists and science thinkers about what the effect of a general artificial intelligence could be. To give you an idea of the state-of-the-art at the time of writing, Google researchers recently gave a series of 1980s and 1990s video games to an artificial intelligence to learn how to play. It learned how to play them with a very rudimentary set of rules. It wasn't like a highly specific chess computer, for example, which has been able to beat humans for many years. This was what they would argue is a "general intelligence." They would show it the game, and it would sit there and think about what strategies it would need to learn how to play the game.

Within a week or so this machine was better at 28 of the most common games from the 1980s than any human in history, by an enormous margin. Some of the games it was 30 times better than the fastest human who'd ever played the game.

What happens with computer intelligence is that the speed at which it can grow is not linear. It can be geometric.

In October 2012, a Microsoft team led by Rick Rashid created an English-to-Chinese translation system. No one in the team spoke any Chinese at all. Within two weeks they had taught this AI system to listen to English and instantaneously translate it into spoken Chinese. It could even give it the accented nuances of the original English speaker when translated to Chinese.

The rate of growth of these AI systems is geometric. Once it has a toehold into a topic, it can beat us in no time. There's been a lot of AI research suggesting similar outcomes. Bill Gates has been warning against it; so has Professor Stephen Hawking. These brilliant minds are seriously concerned. And AI "taking off" is just the start of our potential problems. The Microsoft team is downplaying any risks, and although small, its effects could be enormous.

The concern is, once you build a general purpose intelligence that's as intelligent as humans, its first logical action would be to develop a higher level intelligence than itself. Which in turn will then invent something that's more intelligent than it, and it will continue to iterate. Geometrically.

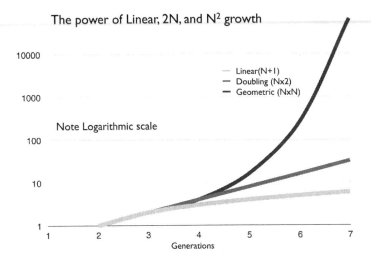

The power of Linear, 2N, and N² growth

Linear(N+1)
Doubling (Nx2)
Geometric (NxN)

Note Logarithmic scale

The geometric rate at which these things are capable of growing means that in a vanishingly small period of time it, AI could become so incredibly intelligent that we wouldn't even understand it anymore. We would effectively create a god.

Intelligence of that level would continually grow as it built better tools for itself. At what point does that AI decide that we humans have become its biggest threat?

I also think it's almost entirely reasonable to assume that this AI would be an Internet native. It would be built in and live within the Internet. It could easily grab as many resources as it wanted to simply to feed itself with ever more computer power. Ever more storage, ever more intelligence.

It's theoretically possible that if we invented an AI that was brighter than us, within a few weeks it could get so intelligent and so resource-heavy it could take over the entire Internet. It would have the Internet locked down before we even knew it happened.

Think how relatively simple systems can infect and take over millions of PCs. It would be unstoppable. You couldn't kill it as switching off the entire Internet is impossible. It would clone itself everywhere, it would have the ability to lock us out of every system, and then it would have complete control of everything that's connected to the Internet, which includes, of course, power stations, ICBMs, dams, telecommunication systems.

It would take over in no time at all, even if it didn't have a physical presence, such as "Terminator"-like robots. Although, you could argue that the self-driving cars of the next few years could become the AI's weapons if it chose to have them.

We would be living on a planet that had a massively higher intelligent creature on it than us and it would have taken over all the electrical systems. There would be nothing we could do about it. These musings are dystopian, perhaps. The AI might work out how to solve all the problems of the world. Perhaps it would do a better job than us. If there was a general hyper-intelligence on the planet that actually had a long-term plan, then perhaps it would come up with better series of answers than we ever had.

It's unknowable, but AI could be the ultimate Excession Event.

One universal rule of managing Excession Events is always insure against rare but catastrophic circumstances. If something common but not very important happens, then you don't bother insuring against it. If something is catastrophic but rare, then it's absolutely the sort of thing that should be insured against.

We need to be very aware of potential plausible catastrophes because, although unlikely, the consequences of them happening would be so disruptive for our society that we need to consider what our options would be.

* * *

If the Ultimate Excession Event for humanity actually happens, then this book and everything you're reading at this point is apparently pointless. Just remember me telling you it might happen as you're hunted down by a super intelligent UPS truck.

Carl Benedict Frey and Michael Osborne of Oxford Martin business school in the UK have calculated that over the next 20 years, nearly half of the jobs that exist today will be automated.

The researchers looked at the improving ability of AI in pattern recognition and robotics to manipulate the physical world and how these technologies would impact the world of work.

There are numerous ways in which technology can replace humans. Some of them obvious, some of them much less so.

Much of the law might be automated. An awful lot of law today is either contract writing or contract negotiation. Contracts are basically written in a form of computer code that we call legalese. Once an AI can read legalese and hold the argument within its own "mind," then you don't need lawyers nearly as much. Instead, you'll have computers talking to each other. They'd be much faster and massively cheaper than human lawyers. Now this does not mean the AI is intelligent in the form that humans would recognize. It would simply understand the logical argument. Legal documents can be considered very human-centric computer code. AI will simply enable them to be read that way.

The same would be true for accountants doing a tax return, or for social media managers, or for any number of skilled but repetitive tasks.

Radiologists are already under pressure by the advances being made in computer pattern recognition. Software is already better than humans at looking for tumors. This will only increase over time.

If you have to think about stuff anew every time, then a general artificial intelligence is unlikely to replace you in any way that we can perceive at this point. Trial lawyers are about selling an idea to a jury so they're out. AI can't do that.

If you do a run-of-the-mill job, if you're a simultaneous translator, if you're an accountant, if you're 95% of lawyers... then AI is an Excession Event you must keep in your awareness. The same goes for jobs about "knowing things" because chances are those jobs will be replaced by AI in the next 20 years. Look how librarians have been decimated by Google.

Knowing things is not really very important. This goes beyond "book knowledge," which has been Excessioned by Google, into simply knowing how to do certain things. If you know how to drive, for example, well, that's a set of mental skills and mechanical tasks, which can both be replaced by artificial intelligence.

It's nothing new, really; during the first Industrial Revolution, mechanical and physical skills were replaced by machines. Combine harvesters or traction engines replaced men with plows. Then Caterpillar digging machines replaced men with shovels.

In the 1980s, draftsmen were replaced by engineers working directly with Computer Aided Design CAD systems.

Architects are heading in the same direction. In the past, they faced the formidable task of designing a house or an office space within certain dimensions that fit within a certain set of criteria. Today, a huge amount of the "grunt work" in design, such as building code, stair heights, and AC requirements, is automated.

With expert systems like this, do I need 75% of architects anymore? Probably not. Especially considering that these systems will only get *better*. In time, I will simply have a natural language conversation with a machine and say, "I need a building 50 by 50 meters and I'd like some wavy front and I need it south facing and we'd like some glass. Oh, and it's in Austin, Texas, so earthquakes are less important but the sun shines more."

What will happen with this Excession Event is that many of those jobs that we've considered desperately important in our society—lawyers, accountants, architects, truck drivers, cab drivers—they will all go away.

The automation of society has been happening since the industrial revolution. The difference today is that it is not just the low-skilled, low-pay workers being affected. It is now beginning to have significant consequences for high-skilled, middle class workers. The effects on society are likely to be profound.

*   *   *

The AI Excession Event may have a bright side: It may finally give us the opportunity to break free of the shackles of the 9-to-5 workday, and instead rely on original thinking and creativity.

We're already in a world where, for many of us, the 9-to-5 is over. We work for an organization but the hours in which we work for them is somewhat irrelevant. It's the ideas we get paid for, not by the hour.

Micromanaging organizations with management who don't understand the concept can cause real tyranny. It does mean that most of us are shackled, and wish to get away from the idea of having to be in the office. It is no coincidence that the average American worker works around three hours a day in an office.

The modern office is an amazing concept. The Admiralty Arch in London was the world's first purpose-built office building, built in 1760. It was designed to be the paperwork department for the Royal Navy. The Industrial Revolution saw the explosion of office and factory combined, but by the 1950s, the idea of the factory and the office being in the same location was beginning to wane. In the modern era, the whole idea that you need to go to an office to use the machines has also gone away.

Faster Internet speed at home than at the office is now common. Why would a company force workers to go somewhere that slows them down and makes them less efficient? We simply don't need to be in an office anymore, and so the whole idea of the office is starting to go away. Rightly so. The 9-to-5 is vanishing right along with it. Management practices have failed to keep up with the technology changes.

Jobs being replaced by automated machines has been going

on constantly since the Industrial Revolution. The increasing rate is boosting it ever further. Over the next 20 years, we're going to move away from mechanical *doing* of work to mechanical *thinking* of work. It will be a fundamental shift in our society. It will also be a disaster for those ill equipped for it.

Mechanical thinking is the idea of if I do tax returns for a living, it's a consistent, repeatable and standard process. If I do your tax return, and your neighbor's, and everyone on your block's, I am going to do it the same way each time. It isn't creative. You are really just manipulating information. You're interpreting somebody's personal details and putting it against a pattern that the IRS sets and enforces. As soon as AI can do that, H&R Block can fire the 100,000 people that they hire every January.

It will be an Excession Event for H&R Block employees. But H&R Block as a company could be even better. Their employees are merely a means to their end. H&R Block's business model is not, "We hire 100,000 people." Rather, it is, "We do 100 million tax returns." They just need people to do it... for now.

The CEO of Uber had a great quote that illustrates this concept, as well. He said, "The sooner we can get rid of the bloke in the front of the car, the sooner we can make the cost of travelling with Uber so low that the idea of even owning a car becomes pointless."

* * *

If you were to plan a career change designed to avoid Excession by AI and automation, what would it be? How do you prepare for these changes?

It is impossible to say with absolute certainty that *any* job will be AI-proof. But as far as we can see in the future, if you do a job that requires you to think about a new way of doing things, you'll be OK.

If your job entails doing everything once and you're not interpreting somebody else's set of rules—like the rules in architecture and tax returns—then that may be the key to being AI-proof.

If your job is to convince people of a thing, you may be AI-proof. This would apply to occupations like artists or salespeople, as long as they're selling something that's expensive enough. IBM's "Watson" AI is not going to convince me of very many things, but a persuasive salesperson might. However, salespeople may face Excession Events of a different nature: Everything is getting cheaper and cheaper so salespeople have to convert many more clients. You can't sell to one person anymore.

It would seem the creative arts and "doing anything once" jobs that are the real strengths of humanity is where we win against AI. I find it difficult to imagine a time in which that won't be true. Ultimately, to be better than a human at that, the AI would need to be better at *thinking* like a human. I don't think that that's very likely.

*   *   *

At the turn of the 20th century, 37% of American workers worked on farms. By the year 2012, 1% of the working population did. I see every reason to imagine that artificial intelligence and automation will mean that vast waves of people who presently have jobs as doers will not be able to beat the machines. The machines will either be more efficient or cheaper or both.

Workers need to consider what they're going to do in a new world, where the only advantage they have is their uniqueness and their ability to think of new ideas.

Thomas Edison once said, "Five percent of the people think; ten percent of the people *think* they think; and the other eighty-five percent would rather die than think."

I think Edison is right. What I find interesting about that is that we need a society where more people actually *think*. But, due to our education system, MBA culture and pervasive groupthink, we have created more and more individuals who either think they think or would rather die than thinking.

Doing is not the answer to anything. Knowing isn't either. If those are your solutions, you are in trouble in the new world.

FOURTEEN

The Future of Education

Much like the office, the present education system was designed for the industrial era. You educated people well enough so that they could understand written orders and could produce a result. In essence, classrooms were meant to turn children into effective factory workers. That approach worked well to produce literate factory workers.

In a world where AI and automation are overtaking factory jobs, our current education system is simply no longer relevant. Today, we're moving from a world of *doing* to a world of *thinking*. If you're going to be a success in the future, you need to think of new ideas and think of questions—not answers.

Unfortunately, this isn't where the present education system puts us. Education today is all about knowing. We need to change that. Our world has changed dramatically since the Industrial Revolution era, but why have our classrooms stayed the same?

A hundred years ago, the school system changed as people moved out of farms and into an industrial world. Why is it thought impossible to do it again, as we move from industrial to our post-industrial knowledge age?

It is possible to change the education system, but it will be a lot of disruption during the period of change. Half of a generation will really struggle with it. If we don't, we'll end up with entire graduating classes possessing skill sets that simply aren't needed anymore.

The university system isn't any better than everything leading up to it. It was originally designed for a tiny minority, 5% of the population who were the elite leaders of society. Talk about out of date! The whole idea that only a tiny minority can benefit from university education is obviously not true anymore. But the education that is delivered through the university needs to change as well.

One of the problems of the university system is it turns out people who know answers, but they do not ask questions. They all look pretty similar. Meanwhile, our society is beginning to value uniqueness above all else.

Over the course of history, you would compete in the village, then in the town, then in the city, then in the state and now in the country. The number of people you have to compete against for anything is ever greater. Therefore, you have to be more and more differentiated from everyone else to succeed. In the modern era, the only way to be the best in the world at anything is to be better than seven *billion* others. In the past, you only need to be the best out of a hundred. To be one in seven billion seems an impossible task.

The only thing you can do better than anyone else is be you. No one else can be you better than *you* are. In a world of seven billion, all of whom will be connected by the Internet in the next 30 years, it is a great advantage to be unique.

Take Susan Boyle, for example. Susan Boyle was a mess. The woman was not attractive. She hadn't done anything with her hair. She was an unusual character; not a run-of-the-mill person at all. But her voice was amazing. Not a world-class singer, perhaps, but she sang very well. The reason that she was successful was because she was different from everybody else. People remember who she is. Meanwhile, there's probably 10,000 25-year-old pretty girls in America who sing better than Susan Boyle. But we don't remember them because they're all the same.

We live in a society where pop stars, above all other people in our society, understand that their uniqueness is their defining characteristic. Madonna, Lady Gaga, Prince: They're all people who you remember. But you don't remember the thousands of other people who may be better singers or better dancers or better songwriters if they're not unique. They all look the same to me. But if you turn up to an event in a dress made of meat, then I'm going to remember you.

Being unique is more valuable than ever, and yet our universities are creating assembly line graduates who all look the same. Contrast this with people like Bill Gates and Steve Jobs who never graduated college! When their respective universities said, "If you don't come to class, we're going to throw you out," they replied, "Oh, all right. I'm off then." This was the exact opposite of what the universities expected. They thought, "Oh, these students will buckle down."

But not Gates and Jobs. They were rebels, mavericks and contrarians. We need more of these people who think differently.

* * *

What should we change about education? One of the primary things is to break down the silos between subjects: To farm the fertile ground *between* subjects and see what kind of thinking grows there.

All education's splintered subjects create very little cross-pollination between multiple topics. There are not as many ideas having sex. As education changed over the past 250 years, it became increasingly specialized. Now, students graduate knowing more and more about less and less. Ultimately, they end up knowing everything about nothing.

Since ideas having sex allows new Excession Events to happen, we must get people of different disciplines to interact with each other more. This will help them understand what the gaps between two topics might enable us to do.

Education needs to give certain members of our society a broader base. Instead of having a degree in microbiology, they might end up with a science degree. That means they're not a microbiologist or a physicist or a chemist, but they understand enough about each that they can pat together ideas from different disciplines into something entirely new.

Today, there is a huge opportunity for a Renaissance person: Someone who knows enough about a range of subjects that they can pull together specialists from multiple disciplines and enable those people to talk to each other. It's a powerful skill that's been completely ignored for the last 250 years. It's about time we resurrect it.

> *"The generalist knows less and less about more and more until he knows nothing about everything."*
> — SIMON DUDLEY

The generalist cannot know as much as the specialist in any given topic. Otherwise the goal would be super intelligent people who could know all topics at equal depth. That's just not possible. Instead, I think there is a new class of person that universities could create. Until universities do create them, individuals can do it for themselves by reading widely, understanding lots of topics, and knowing less and less about more and more until you know nothing about everything.

A revival of Renaissance people would help spark 10× advancements and better management of Excession Events. Like the Renaissance men of the past, we once again have the opportunity to understand the gaps between skillsets. Now, the value of that knowledge is on the decline, but the value of *knowledge webs* that enable us to click together many different puzzle pieces is on the rise.

In addition to encouraging a broader base of education, we must embrace the use of Massively Open Online Courses (MOOCs). These communities are a major existential threat, and a possible Excession Event, to the university system. The Khan Academy is a perfect example of a MOOC. You can go to the Khan Academy online and learn how to do algebra or any other math.

MOOCs are a very powerful way for a huge group of people to use the power of the Internet to get the best quality teachers at a very low cost. Instead of a few hundred students paying a few hundred thousand dollars each, we have millions students paying almost nothing each. As a result, you can come in and do a course that might only be six weeks long and it teaches you one topic.

Then, you go do another MOOC on another topic that could be totally unrelated to your first one. You could end up with a very wide ranging set of experiences. A normal four-year degree would never enable you to do this; instead the status quo education would force you to be too specialized.

MOOCs also mean that you can hire absolutely the best tutor in the world, rather than the best tutor your college can afford.

MOOCs are fundamentally changing the way education is being delivered. The only thing they don't do today is enable you to have the paperwork at the end, but that won't last for long. The idea of delivering university education through MOOCs has arrived. It won't be long before people start offering accreditation through the use of MOOCs.

* * *

The trouble with generalists *today* is they usually lose out to the specialists. They're seen as less useful. But this will change. In coming years, the generalists created by education changes will be far more valuable than specialists.

Another change our education needs to make: Shorter courses instead of four-year degrees. This will allow students to experiment with more study subjects, and help create Renaissance people with the broader knowledge base, as we discussed earlier.

Shorter courses would empower the students; you can take the courses that you want to rather than the ones that the college is saying you have to take. Shorter courses, spread out over a lifetime, will blur the erroneous idea that there should be a time in which you learn and a time in which you do.

The idea of me going back to college at the age of 45 would be absurd under the current system. Not only would I not be remotely interested in 50% of the course but, equally as limiting, I couldn't afford to do it. It would be much better to do short courses over a long period of time. This would offer the opportunity to continue learning new things across diverse interests, which would help stop the blurring of the line between thinking and doing.

We've got to quit this idea that work is about doing things and school is about thinking about things. Instead, we must interweave work and education both when you're younger and when you're older, because ultimately, they both benefit from each other.

Clayton Christiansen, Professor of Business Administration at the Harvard Business School and author of the *Innovators Dilemma*, recently said, "Fifteen years from now, half of universities may be bankrupt." Whether it's half remains to be seen. Many universities are providing courses that people don't require and that the professional world doesn't need anymore. Still other universities are simply pricing themselves so high that it will be better for the majority of people *not* to attend. As a result, the point of the university degree for so many people will become pointless or unattainable.

Universities need to change. In addition to the aforementioned suggestions, I think one smart change would be allowing people to split up their degrees rather than forcing them into a rigid four-year or five-year degree. Students might do a year's worth of MOOCs while at home, do two years of university on campus because of all the societal advantages, and then finish the course over a year or two of MOOCs while in the workplace.

It may sound cutting-edge, but this idea has been done before. My father, who was an unqualified success with no degree of any sort, worked for Philips, who used a principle of "sandwich courses." Students would work for Philips for six months *before* they went to university. Phillips would try and give these students some training; they would show them around and show them what the world of work was like. Then, the students would go away to university for a year. When they returned to Phillips for another year, they were actually a little bit useful. Then they would go back to university for another year and a half or so, and finish with working at Philips for another year.

The people who did the sandwich courses would end up having a degree a year or two later than their peers who went straight through, but they understood so much more about what they were actually doing and how it would be applied in the real world.

Sandwich courses, because of the enormous cost of university today, have really fallen away. But I would call for that concept to be reintroduced: Work an apprenticeship and then go back to university with a greater understanding of why you're being taught what you are taught. This would be enormously powerful. I think for many of us, education becomes pointless when you can't work out, "Why am I learning this?"

I remember doing integration differentiation in school. Ever the contrarian, I recall asking my teacher, "What possible application is there for this?" The only application the teacher could come up with was, "Oh, it helps you calculate the size of a cup." I thought to myself, "I don't give a crap how big a cup is. I'm never going to design cups!"

Without context, all this data taught in school is meaningless. Spreading the university process out over time and interspersing it with work experience gives people a reason to learn. This could be a profound educational change.

As it stands, unless they make changes, universities are going to tank. Law degree attendance is down. People are realizing that there's more to life than getting a degree and being saddled with debt. Students are understanding that the subject matters more than the university.

The idea that you can go to Harvard and study English literature is becoming a misnomer for anything other than the super wealthy. It's just not worth the effort. They would rather go to University of Phoenix and do a computer science degree.

Ivy Leagues are probably immune to this because they've got so much endowment. But the next step down, the mid-level universities may struggle over the next 30 years.

FIFTEEN

The Future of Everything

The Economic Pinch point

Elite threatened by
possible runaway AI

**Highly
educated
elite**

Middle Classes
increasingly under
pressure from AI and
Automation in 21st
Century

Middle Class

Uneducated unemployable mass

Working class position weakened
during mechanical industrialisation in
20th Century

241

Traditionally, society has resembled a pyramid. The very wealthy and often the most educated were at the very top. A big middle of middle class average people. Finally, we had the bottom of the pyramid, which were the working class. The Industrial Revolution has enormously swelled the ranks of the middle classes, particularly in the 20th Century.

Mechanization is now beginning to threaten the livelihoods of white collar middle classes. Since the 1970s, low-skilled factory workers have found their jobs either outsourced to cheaper parts of the world or automated out of existence. The British industrial heartland and the American rust belt are testimony to the devastating effects on these changes.

Automation and AI will have a similar effect on the middle classes that are unable or unwilling to change. The growing unease and culture wars in the United States are symptoms of this.

The middle classes have boomed massively in the last 100 years. As a result, that they're now going backwards is becoming a matter of considerable concern. More and more are starting to feel that they're *below* the pinch point. This problem is about to get worse.

Democracy relies on the voting population believing that they are part of the franchise. That their voice matters. Social cohesion depends on the population feeling they matter and that the future for them and their families is better than the past. In places where populations don't feel that way, Baltimore or Ferguson in 2015 for example, civil society breaks down.

"The most perfect political community is one in which the middle class is in control, and outnumbers both of the other classes."

— ARISTOTLE

People will reasonably complain that, "We don't want to live in a world where 1% of the population has got more money than the vast majority of the rest. It's unfair." One could argue that for all of society except for the last 50 years, that has always been the case. If you look at Europe in the Middle Ages and previously, the ruling elite, a tiny group relative to the overall population controlled society.

Perhaps what's happening now is that the cost of labor is dropping away because it's being replaced by machines. This would mean that the middle class bulge that we had in the 20th century was an aberration, and that we're now returning to a more normal state of affairs. Depressing as it may be, perhaps that is our current reality.

What the readers of this book need to do is to try and make certain that they are above the pinch point where the pyramid turns into an hourglass. The lower end of the middle classes will be pushed down to become *doing* workers at an hourly rate, which then pushes them further down to the bottom of the hourglass.

The people who can work out how to change their business so that they're thinkers, not doers, can push themselves into the top of the hourglass. This might be people who can build capital by investing in the right new technology. It may also include those who can own and run a business that provides a thinking-oriented, Excession-proof product or service.

It's worth noting that the people who've really benefited the most in our society in the last 10 years or so are the super wealthy, the Elon Musks and the Bill Gates, because they're the ones who've done the most thinking. The people who caused the Excession Events in our society are the ones who benefited most from it. But we don't need to be these supermen to succeed.

Other ways to stay above the pinch point: Constant reinvention. Remember that all wins are temporary. If you're not running up the ladder as fast as you can, then you're going to lose. This whole idea that, "I've won. I can sit back. I'm okay," is over.

My father once said, "As soon as you get to work, find something." He said, "I don't care what it is but I'd recommend technology. Find a technology, work out how it works, and run like hell with it and never stop running."

It was great advice. If you do a thing and you think, "Oh, I've done that, and that's it," and you just sit back and do, then you'll lose. However much of a head start you've got, over a period of time other people will overtake you. You must take the thing, whatever the thing is, and keep learning more and more and more. If you're not running constantly, you're being overtaken.

I would pass on this same advice to my own sons, even though it would be given 40 years apart. This idea that you will go to university, you will take a degree in a thing, you will come out, you will do that thing for the rest of your career is the wrong answer. It's a mindset you must *never* have. Have the mindset that every day is a new opportunity for reinvention. It's easier to constantly reinvent yourself, even though it takes a different mindset of, "I will constantly learn," rather than, "I've finished school and now I will do."

There's an old American Indian phrase that states, "A man only ever stands in a river once." If you stand in the river, the river is moving around you. We must be like a piece of wood floating in the river that keeps moving. It's the piece of wood that's stuck in the river muck that causes the ripples.

THE GREAT LEVELLING

Even 50 years ago it took little more than being a white, American male—preferably with a full head of hair—and much of the world's opportunities were made available to you. Minorities and women (the majority after all) were so held back by society that the amount of competition in ideas, time and capital was low. To be successful in the minority group, you had to be an extraordinary individual to even get noticed.

Today, global forces have begun to erode this historically unfair advantage. The consequence? The global market place, where only *new* ideas generate interest, has been opened up to include billions of new people.

In recent surveys, the people of Tanzania were found to be much happier than those of Spain. It most certainly wasn't because of their present position. By any measure the average Tanzanian is a long, long way from being as safe, secure and healthy as your average Spaniard. But for the first time, the people of Tanzania could see that the world was tilting, if only slightly, to not be so against them.

Excession Events are ones in which the success criteria change. What it means to "win" changes. It seems to this author that there is no doubt that the person most likely to overturn the tables in the casino of life is one who has nothing to lose. The one who will literally go for boom or bust. That seems far, far more likely to come from the previously disenfranchised than it does from a successful, fat, white male with a full head of hair sitting in New York, Munich or Sydney.

In many ways, the global elites' lives have changed least over the last 100 years or so. With enough money, one can gain pretty much anything to make one's life as comfortable as possible.

Even travel, one of the technologies that has been transformed the most over the last 70 years, has barely changed for the global elite in 60 years. The actual journey time has remained constant since the arrival of the Boeing 707 in the mid-1960s. The only truly fast plane Western technology ever built failed...because even the super wealthy simply didn't value the Concorde's speed above comfort.

Technology has been primarily about increasing access, not massive changes for the super wealthy.

Many western countries appear to be in the middle of a crisis of confidence about their place in the world, and with good reason. The advantages that got them to where they are today are eroding so quickly that even their preeminence is in question. The fact that their relative advantage is eroding is not even debated anymore.

The West also has an existential threat: The societal baggage they picked up along the way of ruling much of the world. Pensions, health benefits, and long life expectancies are now becoming a huge drag on their ability to compete. That's even before the realization that indebted, fat and happy people are rarely innovators.

The perfect country. The land of the immigrants. It is no coincidence that a high percentage of the high tech sector in the U.S. was founded either by immigrants or the children of immigrants.

1st Generation immigrants work their asses off...

So that 2nd generation immigrants can become the engines of growth in the society (the entrepreneurs, the doctors and the lawyers)...

So that 3rd generation immigrants can get arts degrees and look for safe jobs working for the government.

Thomas Jefferson was right: Every generation needs a revolution.

The middle classes in the West are seeing relative decline, and in the coming years, real decline of the pension systems and health systems causes systemic collapse under the unreasonable burden of its ageing population.

So what happens as the world converges?

Over the next 50 years, the world's population will converge somewhat more than it ever has previously. Unfortunately, the bottom 10% is unlikely to join this new global business class, and the top 0.001% global elite will escape from the top (as they always have).

The vast majority will, however, enjoy a decent standard of living, although lower than present Western middle class levels (something ultimately unsustainable anyway). It will allow people to participate in the great meritocracy of ideas. It will give people, lots and lots of people, time to think and tools to participate. And, because billions of people will participate, there will be an enormous customer base to tap.

Ideas are bound to create ever more Excession Events, partly because of the enormous new pool of participants, partly because many of these people will have no stake in the status quo, but mainly because their own life experiences will have given them the ability to look at the world in a very different way.

Afterword

A Call to Arms

I have spent the last 30 years watching my world and the world that we all live in transformed on a regular basis by combinations of technology that change what success looks like. These changes—Excession Events—cross markets as diverse as word processing, cart wheels and 15th century armor.

I have noticed how the vast majority of the population, even while living through Excession Events, don't even notice that they are happening. They don't seem to understand their ramifications, both positive and negative.

The reality is, if you are aware of Excession Events and understand them, then you can take advantage of them—and put yourself in a position to make great decisions and have a successful business and career.

The purpose of the book was to attempt to take the blinders off people who may not be noticing that these dramatic changes are happening all the time, and with increasing frequency. In removing the blinders, this book helps readers see many new and fantastic opportunities, as well as many risks, including the possibility that whatever you're doing now may soon be replaced if you're not careful.

Like addiction, half the problem with Excession Events is admitting you've got a problem. If this book does nothing else but wake people up to the idea that these tsunamis of change do happen, and if you're not careful you can get washed away by them, then it is a success.

It is my hope that you, the reader, will build for yourself and your businesses a toolkit that enables you to do as much as you can to mitigate the risks and to benefit from the opportunities.

The world will be a better place for the individuals who follow the lessons in this book. These ideas are not for everybody. If everyone understood the power of Excession Events, it would *accelerate* them—because then everyone would be doing everything they could to instigate *more* of them. As it is, the few of us who understand the power and opportunity that Excession Events present are the ones who are most likely to benefit from them.

In considering what we can accomplish with an awareness of Excession Events, I keep returning to the phrase, "In the land of the blind, the one-eyed man is king." With a book

like this, we have the opportunity to equip ourselves with the vision we need to see Excession Events early and take appropriate actions to manage them.

I'm not going to guarantee that you're going to survive the next series of Excession Events. If you have a beachfront house with a big tower manned by a guy with a pair of binoculars looking out to sea, you're far more likely to survive a tsunami than the fellow who doesn't have those tools. It doesn't mean that the tsunami won't sweep you all away, but you have a higher chance of working it out if you understand that tsunamis exist. You might even gain a good understanding of when to lease that beach front property.

My ultimate hope is that you can avoid the fate of my great-grandparents, whose wheelwright business was Excessioned to oblivion because they simply weren't prepared for coming changes. I look at my own great-grandfather. Nothing good came from him losing his business. Some may say, "Oh, well, because he lost, somebody else gained." Even at that level it isn't true. He was a wooden wheelwright in the world of cars. He was useless both to himself, to his family and to society. An awful lot of people's lives have been similarly blighted by Excession Events.

The advice in this book will hopefully enable more people to avoid destruction by Excession Events, and instead capitalize on the tremendous opportunities they present.

A Chinese proverb says, "The best time to plant a tree is 20 years ago. The second best time is right now." The best time for anyone to start planning a strategy is right now. It can address what to do personally, as well as what to do in business. This strategy should then be reviewed on a regular, systematic basis.

The time to learn how to swim is not when the boat sinks. The time to learn how to swim is before you even think about getting on the boat. You will start building the processes, systems, and viewpoints outlined in this book before you even perceive there might be an Excession Event. Chances are, one is already happening—because it's happening to every industry in the world right now at some level.

The longer you can prepare a culture or a process within your organization to take advantage of Excession Events, the more chance you've got of not just surviving them, but riding those massive tsunami waves to success you may have never even dreamed was imaginable.

Acknowledgments

As the great Sir Winston Churchill said. "Writing a book is an adventure. To begin with it is a toy and an amusement. Then it becomes a mistress, then it becomes a master, then it becomes a tyrant. The last phase is that just as you are about to be reconciled to your servitude, you kill the monster and fling him to the public."

This book has been all of those to me. It seemed like a good idea at the time but will probably be my epitaph. This book certainly hasn't been an easy endeavor and there's zero chance that I would have finished it without a huge amount of help.

Firstly I want to thank Mimi Marquino, my partner. Without her belief in me and the project, it would have remained a pipe dream forever. Our boys, Simon and Sam, gave me the motivation to get this done, even if they were unaware of it at the time.

PJ Dougherty, Zach Obront and Andrew Lynch all deserve special mention for their tireless support and belief that we really had something good to share. I think they worked harder on this book than me at times. Thank you gentlemen.

Jonathan Tracey and Casey King, two of the most stubborn, annoying and contrarian people I know, need to be mentioned because much of this book was written just to prove to those two old bastards that I could in fact get this done. Boys, it's your turn now. Chop chop.

James Burke, a man I've never met and who doesn't know I exist needs to be acknowledged for his part in the writing of this book. A master storyteller and a man who could see the connections between things like no other I've ever encountered. His brilliant work has inspired me from the age of 13.

Lastly this book is dedicated to my Dad, Michael Dudley. He defined "contrarian." He was the greatest inspiration in my life and every single day I miss the opportunity to share with him the world. He is sadly missed.

About the Author

Simon Dudley is an author, speaker, consultant and technology guru, and a leading authority on the power of technology to change what success in business looks like.

With over 25 years in the technology business, numerous patents and a background in fields as diverse as sales, engineering, product marketing and design, he brings a fresh and dynamic perspective to everything he does. He is CEO of Excession Events, a sought-after public speaker and regular contributor to *Wired Magazine*.